Published May 2015

INFINITY PUBLISHING
1094 New DeHaven Street, Suite 100
West Conshohocken, PA 19428-2713
Toll-free (877) BUY BOOK
Local Phone (610) 941-9999
Fax (610) 941-9959
Info@buybooksontheweb.com
www.buybooksontheweb.com

Dancing in the Cool Morning Light

Poems and Plays

Richard Alan Bunch

To the memory of my parents

and to

Rita, Katharine, and Rick

With best wishes!

Richard

Oct. 13, 2015

Preface

Throughout this work, from traditional to experimental, the reader will notice continuing experiments with language, voice, imagery, form, diction, rhythm, and so forth. Welcome to these language-experiments, my poems.

Grateful acknowledgement is made to the following editors and publishers in whose publications (including online) earlier or final versions of some of these poems and plays first appeared: *Speedpoets, The Hurricane Review, Brownstone Review, Hawai'i Review, Maelstrom, Orbis, Sonoma Mandala, Poetry Cornwall,* and *Acid Angel. Pele's Lover* was inspired by *The Legends and Myths of Hawaii* by His Sovereign Majesty King David Kalakaua.

In addition, grateful acknowledgment is made to my wife, Rita, for her helpful support, inspiration, suggestions, and also pictures of the author in each of these volumes.

noch nie
war der dichter
so wertvoll
wie heute

(never was the poet so valuable as today)

— Peter-Paul Zahl, "on traveling into exile"

Contents

Poems

Plays

Poems

Late Summer Lament

There you go, faster than those summers past.
Look, this turn too is your difficult path:
Spring leaves, green with spring, already thrown by
Unconscious passages, now hint of autumn
Reds and old undulating magnetisms
Of purples and yellows. You have breezed like
Those swift Basuto ponies in mid-flight.
Your woodlands and swimming hole eddies know
Galloping moons, late suns that rise aglow
With spells of summer runs, bluish rhythms
That explore God as beauty, and believe
Beside pools and these soon-to-be dead leaves.
Your waters cloud with gray bubbles of smoke,
Yet begin their returns through wintry floes.

Coming Home

Trudging home
in the throbbing sunset
from the seashore,
past scallop and mollusk shells
where signs drown
in the blowing sand
that converges
on all four limbs of my body,
I soon hear in the distance
soft and melodious singing
metamorphose
into the glorious lingering
and transfigured sounds
of cha-cha and bossa nova.

Once in my beach house,
I make some green tea,
lie down
and put my feet on the couch,

and wait for a
palomino fist-sized moon
to rise from silent waters.

Doctoring

In fact, there's no need
for fighting
among ourselves
or that revolver strapped
to your head so you may
glimpse a rim of oblivion.

Many streams, of course,
both joy and sorrow,
(the letting go of lovely things)
come to us.

You know that and so do I.

With gratitude, I embrace you
as you are
with your clairvoyant gaze,
divine eyes
that are seascapes forever,
the way your gentle hands
apply medicine.

I tell you, love can win
you over just as
we can still see
the sun upon the hill
after the sun has set.

Time's Weather

We are always travelers
sometimes living on nothing
in a foreign land
where mist rises
from the valleys
and where we can hear
trees grow
with those listening hands.

Here we are born alive
and the divine
with a dormant gene
blossoms in subtle shifts of light.

We realize love is more than this place
where we have visions
of unbleached sails,
snail shells pooled
with time's weather,
the reappearance of minor chords,
and ancestral features in embryos.

Blood Lines

Linked by blood, we make our bed
of earthly dreams of peace
yet we fill the halls of hell
thanks to ruinous seasons
of a work of war I never wanted.

After all the killing, lies,
and mass graves,
I marvel at still living
as I read the morning paper.

Despite advances in weaponry
from the lethal metric
cankers of technology,
summer storms and hail
still try to outrace the wind.

Voices change and even silence does.

Yet there are those who still vow
to serve the sun
in a life beyond death
as their oars row
beneath the shifting shades
of evergreens.

So Far

The future holds the most
remote events
that lean forward
and tumble into novelty
such as finding a road
in white moonlight
that takes me home
to a sleep of borrowed faith,
reconnecting
with my basic humanity again,
noting your desires
in the dark
on a wet sand slate
washed by the tides,
cultivating summer growth
in my green seeming garden,
and sensing earth's passages
against a carpet of stars.

What seems
so far from you
is often the closest.

Finally Virgo

In a Virgo volume
of shamrocks and marigolds
when blackberries hang
under a silent starlit heaven
and above mountains
of primal grief
and distant ocean voices,
there unfolds a bird
with eggshell wings within her.

Finally, she is making love
with the dark one,
the one she longs for,
her perfect love.

In the hush-hush of things,
this is what she was born to do.

New Arrivals

When you arrive,
arrive with affection
and new sounds.

One word of Danish
has changed the whole town.

Outside the window
filled with lemon trees,
you can hear
the rustle
of lilacs and carnations
in our hexagon-shaped garden,
and watch the graceful ibis
and several mallards
in the lagoon.

That is one way
to keep your mind tender
and your nerve-endings simpatico.

And then there is love
that shakes with hopes,
lies, the past of futures,
curls of lips,
and sometimes lethal entanglements.

Keep perspective
and you can avoid
bad seasons for sale.

What you want to do
is end up in the horizons
and maybe, just maybe,
you can envision
the dark face of God.

X=the zoology of love

In the rolling fields,
we know
x=the zoology of love,
from the mating habits
of the yellow-bellied sapsucker
to the spotted owl
to the dormant genes
of ancient embryos.

We also observe
how Eskimos rub noses
and inter-ethnic breeding
occurs in humans
and other mammals.

Yes, you just have
to know the right formula,

expect the unexpected,
and you can be introduced
to the animal kingdom
of this particular world.

Solitary Man

In a season of wild love
next to a wind-swept sea

a solitary man who walks
with Andromeda and Capricorn

whose soul
is no stranger to earth,

turns away from the lairs of lying and
those wastelands of mistaken hunts

and continues to where orchards
of the resurrected meet, and finds

his heart now overflows
with sunrise.

Edda

A fortune teller
once told us
about her and that
we can master the signs
as leaves start dropping
from the Norway maples
while evening comes
on the sea
as the dining room
fills with chatter.

As lightning zaps
down the pages,
she emerges like the heart
of summer between
the man's felicity and fright
while at a distant castle
all the queen's men
joy in the rejoicing.

This shouldn't crimp
anyone's style
as she takes his hand
and deepens the lure
of sleep and dreams.

Tavern Song

Ours a time of memory,
Ours a time of song,

Drink and sing a merry lay
Catch a maid, make a maid
In the hay of May.

Our songs are songs fishers sing:
Tom beneath a moon-bright limb
Dawn a song of memory
John a-hootin' to starry night
Honey a song of love
And Dick a song of joy.

Ours a time of memory,
Time in tune joyfully.

your childhood chasing butterflies

across a paisley field
in them you crown monarchs
of the living dead
and celebrate
the lions of daylight

you come alive
when you are alone
wrestling spites
of time (so intimately
you unearth this
fragile plot) well then
clench the scruff of sky and love!
with cantos of memory

that swell through foraged dreams
they become your playground
of drums and stars

your childhood chasing butterflies
when you find resurrections
in the sculpted past
and the whining of plum wind
down shell shade
wired with all tomorrows
to a clockwise tongue

chasing sounds of butterflies down
lends random
shapes to instant
joy and there
the holy blooms
of madness
yield diviner sense

this ancient rite is
where you
net a tree of wisdom

running suns
down a lizard's tongue
before the dark
begins to plow
the snoring grass

Essays in Divinity

Cherish in yourself
the birth of God.
　　　　　　—Meister Eckhart

What is divinity if it can come
Only in silent shadows and in dreams?
　　　　　　— Wallace Stevens

My last poem lying in the dark;
the nurse has left.
I feel my breathing heavy, my chest
covered with white hair.
Upon me has fallen the hermeneutic
wonder of dreams. In them, I dance

like Zorba the Greek and love women
only God's love can mystically fashion.

Evenings discover me gazing at lines
etched at the Moulin Rouge by my friend,
Lautrec.

In Athens I discuss particulars of
beauty with Plato who hankers for
souls anchored in stars.

On Lesbos, Sappho takes her girls gently
by the arm and teaches them poetry
deeper than a sigh.

Chaplain motored here this afternoon
espousing Christ and his mystic tide.

She also likes the Buddha's flower sermon
that cuts diamonds made of silk. I would

like to take tea with the lady. She does
not wear her badge like the Pharisees: her

Zen sees too far. Her prayers Om.
There is no room for her love of God.

Dreaming, I see life in other universes
and hear restaurants on the moon within

constellations of light years nearest, a
rainbow's genesis surpassing civilization.
Light stabs as curtains part. The
Physician opens my eyes galloping dream,
another pulse!

Dreams have become more real in this

last testament. What we call reality
can be a supremely fictive will, Madame.
A door softly opens:

I hear Neruda in the next age
savoring a breast of his final rose
eternally in flight.

And Tu Fu's brush concentrates:
sunsets magenta as plums inspire

each stroke higher than a man: ageless
ways words mother the fathered heart.

Nearness of end: even here dreams
clarify this orange evening

when the sun also rises
in the shape of Mexico.

The Edge

You have to be keenly aware
of the axe which smells of fur
and blood. You've deluded yourself
into thinking
they won't get rid of you
that you've worked so hard and so well
that nothing like this could happen
to you.

And then one fine day (or night
if they're especially nasty)
you discover we all dangle
in separate skins.
Older blood divorces.
Edges of cordiality
suddenly fold
into stone. Some
friends turn out to be
stillborn after all.

You cringe as you hear the good news.
First your titles, your keys,
next your name, your face,
what little urn of space you occupied,
your worth in money and performance
gone.

You think you've become a dismembered dog
with no opportunity.

It's then that you begin to realize the vast ocean
of the toilet
you've been treading
all these years.

Then it is time for Zen. You remember
the story. Chased by a ravenous tiger
who aches to eat him,

a man finds himself
hanging over a cliff by two vines

being eaten by three mice.
Below, starved lions
wait to devour him.
While hanging, he sees
a wild strawberry. He plucks
and eats it. And it is
so delicious.

Zen Sight

1.

To be the sound of water
is to be between
the sound of white
and whitewater.
No longer to need
to rhapsodize or canonize
the eschatology
of summer trees.

2.

A certain joy shapes
our loneliness
and finally fashions it.
A gateless gate: here
your thinkings crystalize.

3.

Rain beating down on the rain
on an old man in Tennessee;
a parrot cocks her head,
the river keeps flowing.
They all listen

as stars in the fall
fall asleep.

4.

A new way to spoon
eaten thoughts
into a pregnant emptiness:
here, step into this
picture of four pears
on top of a blue mountain,
yes, the one there with
a blue wren on a blue branch.

5.

The work of breeding dreams:
the circular skins of me
and me. How final, how free
the wild swans
in a bleeding twig's kingdom.

6.

By plum trees
the lovers lying
there. And the moon partly hidden.
All together their
lines, which you can barely
make out, map out a sacred space;
centered thus, they all share
the waterfall at dusk.

7.

Nothing exists. Here hangs
a metaphysical tale
on comedians in the dark.
Striking a blue match,
the muscular one plays

a mean jazz guitar
with a clear blue voice
of a sound clearing.

8.

Upon a sun-hammered hill
clusters of knotted oak
paint the true body.
Like trusted habits
shedding snakeskin,
the fallen leaf's
eternity
resexualizes.

9.

Amid parabolas
of soul
and skeins of memory,
a squirrel sits
motionless
as we pass.
Deepening, the river
swirls once again.

10.

As stars skate
across the pond,
a marigold motions
with this aside:
travel light, she says,
*if you wish to approach
the fathomless plum.*

11.

Answer to the riddle
of April rain:

brazened hawks encircle
yellowing flesh
made of yellowing flesh
made of the music of more.

Down To the Sea

People go down to the cobalt sea
even when the sun glides through
fog like a pale foreign disc
over broken driftwood and cooling sand.

They open their minds to resurrections
of sight and mustard suns
and unmask unspoken boundaries
in metaphors of sleep.

With plastic buckets and salted
lips they silhouette hot love
dwarfed against straying spindrift
and knifing oyster tides.

Pelicans and gulls sentinel their islands
as people go down to the orchid sea
evermore down to the sea, the sea,
evermore down to the emerald sea.

Peeling Off

The way sun spatters, spits past irony
through colored glass, or nightfall darkens a round
stone, or how thumbs when stressed blush by degrees—
these voices all hush when your love's risk has flown
downwind and left blue horses of mourning, leaves
stained sorrow, suns made of coal, bleating breasts,
worms for lips, trombones empty, all. You grieve
and rise and bleed and find in each breath death

another of your arts as death's olde thyme
steals the spice of loss, the retrieves of leaves
and engraves on your lonesome homeless charm
a new-borne will's codicil to bequeath:
you pick up your guts and from this cave go
blossom a burnt wisdom who over-knows.

The Summons

We thought you were mad:
a poet has no standing
since you might see something
we would not want to talk about such as
the fury of worms, sleeping breasts,
a plate of bleached skies,
hammering insomnia,
footpaths that eat orange faces,
and blood pistols.

But, alas, we too were a little crazy
so we sat you down
to give you booze and broads
sometimes both at the same time.
Finally, we could say
now you are free to go and
immerse yourself further
in the beauty and follies of the world.

Freight

Much to carry: silks, Muslim
dances in the rawhide sun,
perfumes, rose bushes,
Venetian red tables, mangoes,
horseshoe crabs, sponges,
Norway maples, moccasin flowers,
grapes, bananas, beef tongues,

aluminum, New York ferns,
tiger's eyes, gaffer's tape,
mandolas, whistle flutes,
and apple green jewels.

The crew does its jobs and
when not on watch eat pot-au-feu.
Some laugh and joke at the southern sea
which invites a broken knowledge
that soon resurrects
memories at each port of call.

All these are there when the ship docks,
bringing life to a solitude of books
and the dance of miracles.

Aunt Tyra

My old Aunt Tyra used to say:
"In the spring flowers pick themselves."

I did not know what she meant
by some of the things she would say,
since whatever meaning that came
came to me aslant.

"In the bubbling brooks
of the I
there is an intimacy
of intergalactic space
for I am a rainbow too."

Over the years, I mused
about her words
and then would
shrug my shoulders,
assume her memory was shot,
or she was a poet of some kind,
and hope one day

understanding would emerge
from that yowl of the primal jungle
and I would be able to hew insight
into a delicious
compassion of the heart.

Finally I would make sense
of the beautiful nonsense of her twilights.

Ribbons

Beyond the sierra rim,
a saffron sun rises
and slowly pulls morning out of night.

As skunks eat chickens
and cows and horses graze,
I think of the flesh
of her smoothness
in the expanding emptiness
like a song
that wraps its words
around a silence.

This is no woman
in a dream.

No, love means return
with a rhythm
of lambada daffodils
and rejoicing leaves
in an orchid wind.

We cherish
our ribbon of shared ardor.

The Snowing Art

Horizons of white silence.
A march of seduction.
A new wave of white on white:
Snow falling as though unfallen.

But art layers by contrast
The human tracks
That will not likely restore such waves
No matter how jaded or purple
The footprints, how
Burgundy and mandarin those telling desires
How grayish that innocence.

Larissa

Really, the sound of your heart
is different from those
that sound like
one is passing through
another's as a number
since through the splintered decades
you are now
the Pocahontas park philosopher
with a guessed-at wisdom
as you sample wild grapes.

We know how spices may set
the tongue fox-trotting
and the palate waltzing.

We can taste footprints
of the dancers as they cha-cha
on a marble floor with stunning veins.

"All things leave their markings,"
you say in this ephemeral hour

as you watch the man
across the road in a chestnut tree
and the other one sitting
on a porch in a rocking chair
eating a giant pretzel.

Pregnant

In a world pregnant with purpose
(think *Symphonie fantastique*
and *Finnegans Wake*) and
swept with the colors of dusk,
there are no accidents
when it comes
to the rhythm of lines
that glow like fox-fire in a bog.

Good company helps
the blues evaporate.

Sometimes that is how
light breaks through
life's family tree
whether it is inside mushrooms,
older seaweed,
or in shadows
that move with the wind.

By Chance

In this world where everything
is chance whether it is playing poker,
real estate, banking, making war,
committing murder
and taking revenge,
you have, for instance,
to learn to cut

the thread of revenge
lest a snake
make a nest in your skull.

No, for the sake of honor,
courage, and self-respect
you can, with the passion of summer,
lean toward the light of paradise
in the city of the sun.

That way, you can act well
your part and cultivate creativity
and make, for example,
bohemian sacred art
with its lapis lazuli lakes of sky
and sacred songs
inspired by crystal vases,
make it your lifestyle
to do no harm
so that it zigzags its way
through the house
in the fellow-feeling
of the forest and the sea, or
mapping many passageways
to the caring human heart.

Strangers

Strangers who live here
sometimes drink up
that laboring sound
of a zigzagging morphology
and jeweled memories
of anciently warring families
from interglacial times
to our exploration, often
disguised as love,
of other galaxies.

Stranger that I am,
I open my breast
to this world
with its yellow wild flowers,
plum-scented springs,
dormant genes,
turning and falling leaves,
night-flowering cacti,
and where crickets
endlessly trill.

Dancing Folks

In spite of this stubbornly
closed world
where seeing is often deceiving
and death is a long voyage,
I dance and dance amid the miracles,
including your voice
of vibrant light
and liberating laugh
surrounded by
the graveyard howl
of your infinity.

As I compose this
invisible poem
beneath a rainbow's perfume,
and in dream after lovely dream,
we only know that what lasts
can bring us to a truth
such as this our visible world
is composed of
what we don't know
about the divine.

Gabriella

She took the advice
"Be invisible"
seriously so we were not
astonished by her absence.

In the solitude of winter,
arabesques of math and ballet,
and in the middle
of the flu season,
we still found time to praise whim
and the heritage of pious blood.

We continue to wear our
red blazers and wool skirts
with our innocent look
of popular hairstyles
and dance to loud music
which blasts the woods
that resound to their depths.

Our voices usually glow
to the end of the dark
gray pellets of drying sand
as plowshares work
the heartless hills.

In absence and even in presence,
hers turns out to be
a searching heart
that truly embraces the unfound.

Mountain Climbing

After a long climb up the mountain,
I, who detail my life
on memory alone,
look down

through cloudy mountains
at the flecks of alfalfa
and trees
that drip green seeds
across a symphonic earth.

I think of you, of us.

Had we truly loved in time,
I would not be pondering
the what-ifs of us
by this weeping willow tree
and moccasin flowers.

Though I know
the sun rises for everyone,
my longing for you awakens here.

As I sip more coffee,
cherry blossoms
float by heart
as green stars blink in the distance.

Last Moves

Beginnings always touch
their end
as disclosed by
the last moves of summer
as aging
in the ripening of her face
casts another shadow.

We spend the summer
watering roses
to be resurrected
next spring.

It is not
a symbol of the times
but a toast
to the earth's curves
and the doorless door
season to season
as the wind
kisses those roses of Jericho.

Even a tourist,
that is, a rich vagabond,
may notice this.

As we sip our wine
and live
summer to summer
on the fat of the land,
in the inmost heart's core
our hearts
are still moved by love.

Albion

He leaves his life
among the stars
where one can pay
big bucks
for the illusions
of each day.

Doffing his muscled sleeves,
he no longer cares about empire
or nymphs from the blue grottoes.

Instead, he journeys
through the darkness
across far-flung fields and
beneath the rain's radiant hands.

He dreams and dreams
into the mountains
unshaped by mist
and journeys
until at last
he hugs
a peace and prosperity tree.

Eryn

She is the loveliest
and most learned of angels
even when the sky darkens
with Canada geese migrations
and the sea shouts and hisses
toward a lost gold
and lingering green future,
not to mention
those lightning-flashed moments
of the Pacific.

She is a synthesis
between hibiscus
and the yellow disks of sunflowers.

I love to sleep
in the light of her shadow
for she quickens
the beats of my heart.

That's the way it has been
since the first chaos of things.

Sacré Coeur

As I come into this solitude
and wave to the shore
where vines and bay leaves
embrace and

in the light of sun and moon,
I realize that by God
as salt in water
or a sunbeam reflected
in a pewter dish in Göerlitz,
I live as Christ
broods in all features
such as the skin
over an atrium afternoon.

You and I
may marry at Sacré Coeur
and maybe help
shape the human race
into fragrances of love
among the living.

As the water rises,
I soon notice my pole
a long way down the river.

Poems of Because

Take it from me kiddo
younger selves conceive
poems of because
since a smile is as good
as a volume of myth.

With its rhythmic knowledge
of uncertainties, happiness
floods into my chest
like unforgettable voices
meaningless as the wind.

Here in the home of poetry
a Dutch boy
can kiss
the Buddha's

indexed compassion
as the world touches
a sounding shore.

Life's Own Secret

On beige sand dunes,
as the sun
repeats itself
in the cantos of summer,
you can see
how that ship's bow
scissors the sea like silk.

Easy it is to feel
a distant mourning
for the past that often dies,
not of hunger, but of love,
a newest world in reverse.

Still we seek truth, beauty,
and goodness
for we know justice
is an element of
mothered metaphysics.

Yet the search
is often better
than the finding
as the moon now rises
in evening dress
on a chiton-multiversed sea.

Entranced

In unentranced
habits of the world
orchids are put in jail,
reality enchained,

and without soul,
mind may blast one
universe after another
into ashes of another galaxy.

And yet sometimes,
brothers and sisters,
life can only by dying live.

That is when
leaves rustle and whisper
that time's sunrise dream
unearths a ruddy tongue
of bloom
yellow with
the summers of August
when eternity searches
for out-of-print seasons
and the lips of savannahs.

Angela

After every shower
the silence of flowers
is not only clear and bold,
but a sacred love
for her presence,
tutored by archangels,
lights up the world.

She is wise
beyond our wisdom,
an Olympian in the dark
as she jogs
over grassy mounds
along hands
of the sea
with a summer smile
under the stars.

She touches
our inmost heart
as well as her loves
most near
grass, trees, and wind
in haloes of mist
thinking of water.

Muscle Milk

Singers on spring evenings
inspire the agitation of chords
that fever the blood
as night begins to deepen.

It happens when angels
enter the eyes of lovers
and their muscles of faith
flavored by memory
and flaming visions.

Then as the morning star
breaks from the clouds
and sleeping hands unfold,
the moored boats of dawn gently stir,
Canada geese fly overhead,
and blossoms fall like confetti
and turn the ground
bone-colored and snake-head gold.

Clooney

He is a wild and crazy man
daring a rip tide at his feet
as he listens
to Smetana's *Bartered Bride.*

Truly he adores
how waves hide
in those trade winds
of dreams
as they rasp across
ice plant and grassy dunes
and how they wobble
the web-scrolls of spiders
in French vanilla sea breezes.

He knows bliss happens
where currents gush
and on the dark side
how passion
makes a display of us
as lovers unbutton lovers.

Aloha Oe (Until We Meet Again)

for my sister

Sweet Leilani, heavenly flower,
angelic bloom that bloomed
and grew among us
your petals reaching out
with care to others
beyond yourself and
tenderly touching
and teaching so many in the family.

We had you for awhile
and count ourselves blessed.
The history of life,
we know, is the history of disease.
We watched you fade and now
will bloom once again
among the angels
that welcome your service
above yourself

in their community
where you will bloom forever.

Aloha Oe
(Until We Meet Again), Lani

Denise

While sitting beneath
the genealogical roof tree
and whispering a prayer
to the masks
of future centuries,
the chittamwood tree
oozes pink blush
among the oaks.

That evening
at the Blue Cue Café
listening to Sting's *Fields of Gold*,
I realize how twilight
takes the sting
out of her sad eyes
and musings on death.

Truth dawns on me
like a beer-bright Van Gogh
and stuns my nose
like the bouquet
of magnolias in bloom.

Because my life
falls in spring waters over her,
I praise Venus
who grants me time
to revel
in the exciting simplicity
of her hip body.

True Wars in Our Town

Amid the rhythmic maracas
of a Mexican fiesta
Michiko's blue blood
changes to black
in each artery
while we eat tuna fish sandwiches
and read from *Animal Farm.*

Mobs of crying fawners
hooked on ecstasy
greet cartel drug dealers
alongside soft-scissored sea foam
as sea winds help blow away
the whorehouse stenches
amid the lie of sleep
and copulative language
while birds tune
their morning joy
beneath clouds
that blot out the sun's glare.

Nuggets of joy
and kisses of death
mushroom here
depending on
what you are looking for.

Billiards

We talk next to the branch
of a plane tree
and gaze at a delft blue harbor,
sun mountains, and then
slide our fingers
over the voluptuous braille
of twelfth century stone walls.

After all the traumas
you have been through,
you say you are finally at peace,
a peace that
secretes a mushroom path
to the brain,
a taste of forever with each breath.

In the changeable currents
of fading water colors,
we play billiards
beneath fish bones
of the moon until it is bedtime.

And before long
hair melts into dark
in sleep's luminous land
where the teasing wheels
of dreams turn and return.

Uncalled-for

In an uncalled-for land
there emerges urban forests
with walls overgrown with scales,
African nonsense
of turning young with rain,
callous faces of people,
urine-stinted trees,
deep gulfs between people
as the mind becomes a prisoner.

But here shady trees
extend our days,
fields of bleached chips
and summer sand,
calyx-shaped breezes off the lake,
roofs that talk together,
and celebrate
the vast incubator

that is the universe
where we can listen
to wild ones
in the wane and wax
of the banjo world.

Jersey Bell

Lounging in his bentwood chair
on a sun-chevroned porch
and beneath a boxing monkey,
he listens to Rihanna's
album *Good Girl Gone Bad.*

No longer deprived of memory,
he cherishes cascades
of unearthly music
that explodes in vibrations
as his soul emerges from darkness.

After tasting pears
marinated in red wine,
he realizes he prefers,
with a mariner's
clever certainty,
the living heart that presses
out a deathless wine.

Whangdoodle

Next to a groundswell
of blue sea blue
foothills to hollers
there is a lake mirrored
with clear water.

It happens during
a summer festival
in the guise

of green calligraphy:
you discover,
on or off campus, that is,
the home of little while,
that you can be
as you have chosen to love.

The moon glimmers
in darkness
as it hugs the window pane.

We begin a dream
and even experience
occasional insight
during the humming
noises of a whangdoodle.

We hug those we love
as does the moon
near that cliff-deep leeward coast.

Bolero

In the whiskey-colored light,
sea fog clouds
in the apple trees
that branch
like a kinetic turning
of malaguena music
much as a clock hand ticks
with a text message
spliced with riddles.

A rainbow shares
its deep violet
with a chickadee,
a wind from the dairies,
and a fish's grey gills
that navigate the truth
as to why the lynx lurks

by fences scratched
with dried blood.

Styx

Some get into bed with the lord
while listening to
the Raj Umber Trio
or Verdi's *Don Carlos*
and become leaping puppets
of a misunderstood dream
and with murdered petals,
end up with
too much time on their hands
as they navigate the
tickling river Styx.

We know amorous night,
inflected by awareness,
argues in darkening clusters,
discarded trojans,
and footing
in the kiss of an old frontier.

This goes on
as autumn leaves
flutter and fall while
gravity tugs light
among the angel
insects of late summer.

Cabo

Tired of the desolation of reality,
the fury of human veins,
and the doctored debris
of imploded day,
and that lovers

die many times
while they live,
and taste wandering scents
among murmuring
mulatto mountains
and nights as blue
as Cabo San Lucas.

Here sandpipers
are dazzled
by the dazzling
yaw of the sea
amid the dream
of enchanted islands.

The lovers use studs
for rosary beads,
dance with ferocity,
keep promises,
and breathlessly
vow beneath riftless stars.

The Future of Nostalgia

We can see ahead to treasure
ancient unchronicled nostalgia
for the times we ran
with the hands
that feed golden dreams
and caroled songs
where no one dies.

This despite a world where guns,
bombs, and fire happen
as a droned narrative.

Sometimes we need an escape,
however brief,
to recall as the wind

shimmers though the pines
how the swallow brings back
blades of grass,
the vase of coral tulips on the sill,
and the way a fisherman
lets down his line in the current.

We can create
another reality just for relief.

Psst!

Under this crucifix,
let me tell you about
my earliest recollections
as I contemplate the void.

One was blowing bubbles
that flowed pink
from a coral throat.

Another one was
discovering a wildwood
in an axe
beneath the sky's roughcast
amid the printed silk
and aromas
of tropical orchids.

A third one was uncovering
the secret ingredient of love,
namely the fusion
of absence and presence,
a fire smoldering beneath
the lovers' ball,
a whirling madness
that escapes shingle-cracks
of light
in every house in our town.

Nobody

In a garden made by fire and time
there is a statue
displaying a gold patina.

As he works in the garden,
weather moves upon his mind.

"Where is the summer
that lasts forever?" he asks himself.

He tries not to be surprised
by his daily perusal of weather reports.

Etched on the statue read the words
"Nobody made us possible."

He pauses to ponder those words.

Perhaps unwed girls, porn stars,
or votaries that body forth
a man and a woman.

He summons energy
to finish his work
beneath branches
feathered with green.

Once finished, he plays solitaire,
drums the piano wood
of his Yamaha,
and sips Grgich Hills Chardonnay.

Now he is ready to play
The Shadow of Your Smile
and *Kadota's Blues*.

Plays

Pele's Lover

A Play in Three Acts

CAST

Pele	Hawaiian goddess of volcanoes
Hiiaka	Pele's sister
Lohiau	a prince of Kaua'i
Atiu	an elder on Kaua'i
Pauo-palae	Pele's servant
Omeo	1st old woman
Uli	a demon
Papau	2nd woman
Tiki	crazy man
Olepau	king of Maui
Waihimano	queen of Maui
Ulani	a seer
Keoni	a messenger
Piglet	a wild boar
Paoa	Lohiau's high chief in Kaua'i
Konane	Lohiau's chief navigator
Milu	king of death and the spirit underworld
Kanemilohai	divine relative of Pele's family

Forests populated by fairies and gnomes as well as nymphs and monsters guarding streams and rivers. Also there are royal guards and Pele's other sisters and brothers.

Act I

Scene 1

The coast of Puna

PELE: (to Hiiataka) Isn't it fun to assume human form? Now we can surf to our heart's delight.

HIIAKA: And now we gather edible seaweed and squid.

PELE: I think I'm going to relax in the shade of this hala tree disguised as an old woman.

HIIAKA: Good idea. Everyone seems to be having a great time.

PELE: I'm going to take a nap. Don't let anyone or anything disturb me.

HIIAKA: Your wish is my command, sister.

[Pele gets comfortable and closes her eyes. In a moment she opens them.]

PELE: What is that sound? It sounds like drums. A rhythmic music.

HIIAKA: I don't know.

PELE: I'll assume my spiritual body. You keep watch over my human body while I find out the source of that beautiful music.

[Pele vanishes.]

[In a few moments, Hiiataka hears from Pele.]

PELE: Are you still watching over my mortal body?

HIIAKA: Of course, sovereign sister.

PELE: Good.

HIIAKA: Have you found the source of that music?

PELE: After speeding to Maui, Hawai'i, Moloka'i, and O'ahu it was still farther away. But I finally found it on the beach at Kaena on Kaua'i. I'll let you know what I found.

[Pele vanishes again]

Scene 2

Kaena beach on the island of Kaua'i

PELE: (aside) (I think I'll assume the form of a beautiful woman among all these musicians, dancers, and crowds of people.)
[The people immediately note the presence of Pele's charm and features as she makes her way through the crowd. Pele finally sees the source of that music in the person of Lohiau, the handsome prince of Kaua'i, who is playing the hula drum of his favorite deity, Lakakane.]

PELE: (aside) Beautiful music, an exquisite dancer, and very handsome too.

LOHIAU: (muttered under his breath) She is more beautiful than any women on this island.
[He goes and sits next to Pele and is obviously enchanted by her beauty.]

LOHIAU: You are most welcome but I am sad that you have come.

PELE: Why is that?

LOHIAU: Because until now I thought Kaua'i had the most beautiful women. After seeing you, their faces look plain indeed.

PELE: Ah, I see you know how to flatter women too.

LOHIAU: Not better than I know how to love them. And if I say that you are as beautiful as I say you are, then you have no reason to doubt my sincerity.

PELE: We shall see what we shall see.

Scene 3

Lohiau's palace

[After weeks of festivities including hula dances, Pele is convinced of Lohiau's sincerity.]

LOHIAU: Have you enjoyed the dancing and the festivities of the past few weeks?

PELE: It has been sheer delight. All the fish, especially the humuhumunukunukuapuaa from that hukilau and the roast pig, poi, and drinks, including coconut milk. What more could one want? You are quite a hula dancer and drummer, my prince.

LOHIAU: You said 'my prince.' Am I your prince?

PELE: Indeed you are. I am now convinced of your sincerity.

LOHIAU: Then we can marry?

PELE: Your sovereign wish is my command, oh prince.

LOHIAU: (calls his people together) You men prepare a wedding feast with all the gifts, music and dancing for Pele and I are to be married.

[The people and Lohiau's other wives applaud and congratulate the prince's newest wife.]

Scene 4

[They pledge their love together; Lohiau pens a love poem to Pele and Pele is also deeply in love with Lohiau and tells him so; they live happily until she must return to Hawai'i and her sister Hiiaka who is still guarding her spirit body on the beach at Puna]

LOHIAU: I cannot put adequately into words the love I have for you. I have tried to express it in a poem but I am no poet so please do not be offended if you do not like it.

[He reads a poem called "Shoreline"]

Shoreline

Along the shore
with its conch shells and feathers,
the sea's dominion
ignites thoughts
of my love in its spray.

My love for you
happens in the cavity of dreams
and intimate rendezvous of night.

It makes me want
to converse with serpents,
kiss the grapes
that are your lips
and lionize the sweet fragrance
of your love.

PELE: Oh, that is so beautiful. You are a wonderful poet and I love you so.

LOHIAU: These past few weeks have been like living in a dream.

PELE: I could not be happier. This time has been so wonderful and to be married to a king. But I must return home to Hawai'i. I still have much to do there.

LOHIAU: What? You don't have to go. You're my wife and my love. Please don't go! Please stay!

PELE: I'll be back in no time. I have much to attend to.

LOHIAU: I don't believe this. Now you're off to Hawai'i.

ATIU: [For the past few weeks Lohiau has refused his food and has now died of grief since Pele left.] Love is that powerful. Yes, it is.

Act II.

Scene 1

The coast of Puna

PELE: Thank you, Hiiaka, for watching over my mortal body. I hear the natives have been watching too.

HIIAKA: Yes they have. They were wondering why you were gone so long. The fires of Kilauea have almost gone out from neglect.

PELE: Well, let me describe my adventures on Kaua'i.
[As Pele describes her adventures, Hiiataka has her mouth wide open at times with surprise and awe at her sister's description.]

HIIAKA: You were married too? And he died of grief?

PELE: Apparently so. And that's what I want to talk to you about.

HIIAKA: Me? About his death?

PELE: (nods) I'll confer on you some of my powers such as bringing him back from the dead. Bring him back to me. I'll send Pauo-palae here to go with you. I trust her prudence and wisdom. She will be a wonderful companion and servant.

HIIAKA: Ok. Are you in love with this mortal, Pele? Remember, he's just a mortal.

PELE: Let's put it this way. He's been hard to forget.

HIIAKA: (nods) I kind of understand. We'll travel as mortals. Let's go, Pauo-palae.
[They make their exit.]

Scene 2

(a forest near Hilo)

HIIAKA: Who goes there?

OMEO: I am but an old woman taking this hog as a sacrifice to Pele.

HIIAKA: Oh, I'm sure Pele will be pleased.

OMEO: Could I follow you? I won't be any trouble.

49

PAUO-PALAE: (she and Hiiataka exchange looks) All right. If you won't be any trouble. You can come along.

OMEO: I'll take this hog to the crater. Be right back.

[They continue their journey to Hilo. Before long a demon named Uli threw himself across their path an attempted to destroy them.]

OMEO: A demon! How big and hideous looking!

HIIAKA: (quickly) Let me call my brothers to get rid of him.

[In moments, thunder can be heard.]

OMEO: That should do it. He's gone back to his den in the hills.

HIIAKA: That's where he belongs. Let's go on.

OMEO: Now who is this?

[A second woman appears.]

PAUPAU: Where are you going?

HIIAKA: To Hilo.

PAUPAU: Can I come with you?

OMEO: Okay. Follow along.

[They proceed a short distance until they meet a crazy man named Tiki.]

TIKI: (flailing his arms and jumping up and down) Agaagaaga ooooga ugaaaaa egaaaaa oooooga!!!

OMEO: What a ferocious-looking man!

PAUPAU: (with a look of horror) An evil spirit! I'm going!

[She runs away.]

TIKI: ooooooga egaaaaa agaaaaaa igaaaaaaa!!!

OMEO: Doesn't look like he's going to attack us.

HIIAKA: No, he doesn't. Let's just go on.

[They continue on their way to Hilo. Tiki gradually fades behind them.]

OMEO: That woman just fled. What a coward.

HIIAKA: I just turned her to stone for her cowardice.

OMEO: Serves her right.

[They continued.]

PAUO-PALAE: We can't cross here. Something's backing the water up.

OMEO: It's a giant alligator. Looks like forty feet long!

PAUO-PALAE: And huge eyes. He's opening his mouth to eat us.

HIIAKA: I'll take care of that. Open wide. Here's a stone for your big mouth.

[She throws a stone that becomes red-hot when it touches his throat and a scream can be heard as he disappears down the river.]

OMEO: That's one gator that won't bother anyone now.

HIIAKA: We're now at Honoipo.

PAUO-PALAE: Look everyone's surfing.

HIIAKA: And I'm in a trickster mood. I'll turn their surfboards into stone.

[She does so.]

OMEO: Look, they're screaming and running away.

HIIAKA: Probably thought some sea-god was ready to devour them.

[Her companions nod in agreement.]

OMEO: Look, a fisherman in his canoe.

HIIAKA: (with a sly smile) I'm still in a trickster mood.

OMEO: What are you going to do?

HIIAKA: I think I'll attach his hook to a sunken human head.

[She does.]

PAUO-PALAE: He's bringing his line in. He thinks he has a fish.

OMEO: He's brought the skull in.

PAUO-PALAE: He looked at it a moment and with a look of horror he is paddling away.

[They all laugh.]

Scene 3

[They are outside the palace of Maui King Olepau.]

OMEO: What a beautiful palace!

PAUO-PALAE: On a beautiful island!

HIIAKA: Wait. The king is on his death bed.

OMEO: Really. How appearances can deceive.

HIIAKA: It's the king's half-freed soul. Here let me tie it to my skirt.

[Despite palace guards who hold back their spears, she knocks on the palace door.]

WAIHIMANO: Yes, who are you?

HIIAKA: Your husband, King Olepau, has just died.

WAIHIMANO: He has not died. I know because the two lizard gods I worship have assured me he would recover. He is simply sick.

[Hiiaka and her companions travel on.]

WAIHIMANO: (consults a seer) I just returned to the palace and my husband is dead. A strange woman told me he had died and I did not believe her.

ULANI: That was the sister of Pele who had come to heal your husband. But you insisted he would recover.

WAIHIMANO: What can I do?

ULANI: Fetch a pig as a sacrifice and maybe, just maybe, she will return and bring your husband back to life.

WAIHIMANO: (to a messenger) Go get a pig and give it to Pele's sister if you would save the life of your king.

[The messenger named Keoni goes and gets a pig that starts squealing and oinking.]

WAIHIMANO: Follow them with the pig.

ULANI: Will do, your majesty.

[They proceed in the direction of Hiiaka and her companions.]

HIIAKA: I'll be with you in just a few moments.

[Her companions continue on.]

HIIAKA: I'll disguise myself once again as an old woman. No one will recognize me as Pele's sister.

[Enter the messenger who looks around, shrugs his shoulders and goes back to the seer.]

KEONI: I saw no one matching the description of Hiiaka. I only saw an old woman so infirm she was scarcely able to walk.

ULANI: You fool! That old woman was Hiiaka in disguise. Hasten back to her if you would save the life of your king.

[Keoni again heads in Hiiaka's direction but the pig is stubborn and troublesome and his progress was slow.]

KEONI: Come on. You're so stubborn.

PIGLET: I don't want to go, to be another sacrifice. I have my pride.

KEONI: And you'll be delicious when roasted underground.

PIGLET: Not a chance. You humans don't even appreciate our intelligence. You just think all we do is oink and grunt all day. We're actually very sensitive.

KEONI: Brother, I've heard it all. Pigs are sensitive. Hmmph!

PIGLET: (with pride in his voice) We truly are.

KEONI: Here, I'll carry you.

[He runs until he is within sight of the women.]

HIIAKA: Let me strike my skirt against a rock and now we can say King Olepau is truly dead.

OMEO: Serves the queen right. How stubborn!

Scene 4

(Honolulu on the island of O'ahu)

OMEO: I just love the beach here. Waikiki.

HIIAKA: The gentle waves washing the sand.

OMEO: Popping breakers.

HIIAKA: Sunlit palms.

OMEO: Oh, and look over there. Diamond Head. Looks to me like a tuna's dorsal fin.

HIIAKA: Sure does. No lava flow there.

OMEO: That's right. An extinct volcano.

HIIAKA: Now you see why I cannot neglect volcanoes. Well, we had better sail on to Kauai.

Scene 5

(Kaena on the island of Kaua'i)

HIIAKA: I see Lohiau's spirit hand beckoning from that cave among the cliffs. We have failed. Pele's lover is dead.

OMEO: I'm so sorry. And to have traveled all this way.

PAUO-PALAE: What should we do?

HIIAKA: (to her companions) You all go on to Puoa where Lohiau's body is lying in state. I'll go rescue the spirit of Lohiau being guarded by two demons, the lizard women Kilioa and Kalamainu.

HIIAKA: Listen up. I'm taking the spirit of Lohiau. Don't you hiss at me! No more hissing, I tell you.

HIIAKA: (aside) One wave of my skirt and they will leave. [She waves her skirt and the hissing demons disappear.]

HIIAKA: Now to find Lohiau's spirit.
[She takes a moment to search.]
Aha, there it is in a niche in the rocks. Probably placed there by a moonbeam. Here I'll put his spirit in a fold of my skirt and we can float in invisible form down to Puoa.

Scene 6

The chamber of the King of Death

HIIAKA: It's after nightfall. Now I can enter the chamber of death unseen and restore the spirit to Lohiau's body.

LOHIAU: (looking around in amazement) What's this? [He touches his head, legs, and arms.] Am I alive? What *is* this? He raises his head.

GUARD: (with a frightened voice) Let's get out of here!

HIIAKA: (suddenly appears in mortal form)
[She holds up her hand as if to command obedience. The guards stop their flight.]

HIIAKA: Fear nothing. Say nothing of this to anyone. Lohiau has returned to the living and if properly cared for may recover. His body is very weak. Let his body be secretly moved to the seashore. Since it is nighttime, it can be done without anyone seeing you.

Scene 7

A hut by the seashore

HIIAKA: (to Omeo and Pauo-Palae)
  Along with the herbs, don't forget the chants, and
  the hula. I'll do the massages.
OMEO: And many prayers for him.
HIIAKA: (she chants one she learned from O'ahu)

  Fragrant Puna is dancing in the wind
  Dancing are the hala groves of Keaau
  Dancing is Haena with Hopoe
  Dancing are the women by the sea of Nanahuki
  A dance of joy by the sea of Nanahuki
  A dance of joy by the sea of Nanahuki

  [A few days later.]
HIIAKA: (to Lohiau)
  You're looking well.
LOHIAU: You all have been so kind. The chants, herbs,
  prayers. (to Hiiaka) And your massages I won't
  ever forget.
LOHIAU: (to his people) I'm alive again today and
  restored to health thanks to these lovely people.
VOICE FROM THE CROWD: How did this happen? We
  thought you were dead, your majesty.
LOHIAU: I owe to the gods my return to life. That's all
  I can tell you. In the meantime, let us have some
  feasts and I will make sacrifices to the gods,
  including Lakakane and Pele.
  [A few days later.]
LOHIAU: (to a gathering of chiefs) I will going to Hawa'i
  to visit my wife, Pele. In my absence, I am leaving
  the government in the hands of my high-priest
  and friend Paoa. I expect all of you to give him the
  respect and fealty he deserves.
  [The next day Lohiau and his companions,
  including Hiiaka, Omeo, Pauo-Palae, his chief
  navigator, high priest, personal attendants

embark for Hawai'i in a double canoe bearing the royal standard.]

LOHIAU: How long do think it will take us to get to Hawai'i?

KONANE: Maybe a few hours. It's a nice day for sailing.

HIIAKA: It certainly is. The sun is shining and the sea is calm.

OMEO: It's almost a perfect day for the returns of life and love.

HIIAKA: It certainly is, especially the return of love.

OMEO: Sometimes love that returns is love returned.

HIIAKA: That's usually a delightful situation, especially love that is returned.

OMEO: And love that is returned in unusual ways.

HIIAKA: And unexpected ways, Omeo. Unexpected ways.
[They finally reach O'ahu.]

HIIAKA: Finally here at the top of the Kaala mountains.
(she looks over at Hawai'i and a frown comes on her face)

What has happened? A lava flow has destroyed my seashore retreats of the hala and lehua groves near Puna beach. (aside) This does not look good. Something's wrong. This is awful. I fear one woe after another. I'd better get back to my companions, including Lohiau.
[She rejoins her companions.]

HIIAKA: Oh, the beauty of the Kohala coast, fit for royalty!

LOHIAU: (to his servants and attendants) All of you stay here while Hiiaka and I head for Kilauea to visit my wife Pele.

PELE: My sister gone for so long in Kaua'i. I just know she fell in love with Lohiau. Jealousy can have an element of rage in it. Hiiaka's friend, Hopoe, is just the beginning. I will teach my sister a lesson in rage.

HIIAKA: Oh, no. My dear Hopoe what has happened to you? You've been tortured by volcanic fire and now you are turned to stone. It's Pele's rage.
[They approach the crater at Kilauea.]

56

HIIAKA: (aside) I am a little frightened by what Pele will do. (to Omeo and Pauo-Palae) You two go ahead and announce to Pele my return with Lohiau.
[She stands in front of Pele.]

OMEO: Your majesty, Hiiaka has arrived with Lohiau.

PELE: (with almost a growling sound) I order the two of you to be killed at once. (aside) Lohiau will suffer the same fate.
[Royal guards take both of them away.]

HIIAKA: (throws her arms around Lohiau's neck) I must tell you of my sister's rage and that she plans to have you killed. And I am sorry. I truly am. I bid you a fond farewell for you are truly a wonderful prince and I am so proud to have known you.
[Pele has watched this whole scene.]

PELE: (enraged beyond measure) How touching! Lava, o lava flow between them! And now the destruction of Lohiau by fire! Blaze and blaze until he is gone!
[Pele's sisters ascend the crater to execute Pele's orders.]

LOHIAU: (chants a song) My love, oh my love, I am innocent, yes I am, and plead for your mercy, for I am innocent, yes, I am, my love.

PELE: (her rage now rekindled) Plead all you want. You betrayed my love! I'll hear none of it!
[Pele's sisters pity Lohiau and touch the palm of his hands which turn to lava. Then they leave.]

PELE: I saw that. Get back here and touch him everywhere so he turns completely to stone. Unless, of course, you want to be punished for your disobedience.
[The sisters return to Lohiau at once to finish their work of destruction.]

LOHIAU: Please, oh please, Pele. Please spare me!
[The trees are so moved they weep with grief.]

PELE: I don't care if the trees are weeping with grief. I command you to continue the work of destruction!
[The sisters begin again the work of destruction. They touch his breast, knees, thighs, and feet which turn to stone.]

HIIAKA: (aside) I still have the power Pele gave to me to make Lohiau's body not feel any pain. There. At least he won't feel any pain as his joints turn to stone. (to Lohiau) Listen! When you die go to the leeward side of the island and I will find you!
[The next moment Lohiau was a lifeless pillar of stone.]

HIIAKA: Okay. Earth, I command you to open at my feet. [The earth opens.] Now down the five spheres, to the realm of spirits presided over by Milu, the king of death. Maybe I can overtake the soul of Lohiau. [She now stands in the presence of Milu.]

MILU: Welcome, Hiiaka, or should I say your majesty, to my dominions.

HIIAKA: Thank you for welcoming me, Milu.

MILU: What, may I ask, is the occasion that brings you to my realm?

HIIAKA: I want to know if the soul of Lohiau has arrived here yet.

MILU: No, not yet. I'm sure he'll be here soon. You can wait here in my realm as long as you need to.

HIIAKA: Thank you for your kind invitation. I'll do that.

Act III.

Scene 1

The island of Kaua'i

PAOA: (to the people) You've all heard the story. How our beloved Lohiau was destroyed by Pele and turned into a pillar of stone. Well, I am enraged by such a fate and I plan to go to Hawaii and denounce Pele for what she has done to my royal friend.

ULANI: Aren't you afraid for your life if you do this?

PAOA: It will be a noble death for such a fine prince as Lohiau. I really don't care what she does to me.

ULANI: You will be destroyed instantly. She has that kind of power.

PAOA: Then so be it. Make ready to go. Now.

Scene 2

The beach at Puna and on Kilauea

PAOA: This may be the last time to see Kilauea, but I determined to denounce her.

[They ascend the walls of the crater.]

PAOA: Here's my sacrifice to you Pele! Enjoy these rocks and cactus! Put that in your flowered headdress, you white dog. All you and your volcanic deities are nothing but evil! Take that, you evil spirit! Enjoy these palm tree branches and more rocks you fire goddess of evil! May your sister enemy, the goddess of the sea, swallow you up.

[He stands there waiting to be instantly destroyed. Although Pele's brothers and sisters were ready to destroy Paoa, there was a long pause.]

BROTHER #1: I've never heard anyone have the audacity to dare to denounce Pele.

SISTER #1: Especially coming from a mortal tongue!

BROTHER #2: You know swift vengeance is on the way!

SISTER #2: What is our sister waiting for?

SISTER #3: Let's get it over with.

BROTHER #3: I agree. I'm tired of waiting.

> [Nothing happens.]

PELE: All things considered, I am now convinced of the innocence of Hiiaka and the fidelity of Lohiau. They shall be forgiven. (to her brothers and sisters) Bring this mortal to me.

> [They go and get Paoa who struggles vainly against them.]

PELE: I welcome you in friendship Paoa. In fact we all do. I can do without your defiance, not to mention your insults and repulsive offers of sacrifice.

> [Paoa is gripped by surprise and bewilderment.]

PELE: I forgive your offenses. As I said, I welcome you in friendship.

> [Paoa is no longer bristling with anger. His surprise maps his face.]

PELE: I have done a great wrong to my faithful sister Hiiaka and would love to have her again dwell with me in Kilauea. I'll bring back Pauo-palae and Omeo back to life.

> [She brings Pauo-palae and Omeo back to life.]

OMEO: Am I alive?

PAUO-PALAE: I think we both are!

OMEO: We sure are!

> [Pele now speaks to Omeo.]

PELE: Omeo, I will endow you with powers that will allow you to enter the kingdom of the dead to persuade Hiiaka to return to earth. Will you do that for me?

OMEO: Of course your majesty.

> [She descends through the opening made by Hiiaka. Soon she is standing in Milu's kingdom.]

MILU: Yes, what is the occasion of a visit by a mortal?

OMEO: I have come to persuade Hiiaka to return to the earth on the orders of Pele.

MILU: (aside) I am not anxious to have such a distinguished guest as Hiiaka leave now.

> [He speaks to Omeo.]

She has already returned to earth and, if I remember correctly, she is visiting some of the relatives of her family in Kahiki.

OMEO: Oh, I didn't know that. But I'm glad she's returned to earth. I guess I'll leave and return too.

[She leaves.]

MILU: (smiling) Understandably. Have a safe trip.

OMEO: I'm disappointed in not finding Hiiaka but it is hard finding someone that has already returned to earth.

[As she readies to leave, she is surprised to see Hiiaka emerging from a grove of trees.]

OMEO: I heard you had already returned to earth.

HIIAKA: Who told you that?

OMEO: Milu did. He said you already returned to earth.

HIIAKA: He's obviously a liar.

OMEO: Well, I was sent here by Pele.

HIIAKA: (with a puzzled look) Why?

OMEO: Now she understands that you are innocent and sent me to persuade you to return to earth and rejoin your relatives in the crater.

HIIAKA: If that's what has happened, let's go.

[They ascend through the various spheres to the earth.]

PELE: Welcome home, Hiiaka, my loving sister! And you have my loving affection again, my sister!

[Pele and Hiiaka hug each other.]

BROTHER #1: What a joyous occasion to have you back, Hiiaka!

SISTER #1: I couldn't be happier!

HIIAKA: No one more than I!

[Hugs all around.]

HIIAKA: (sees Paoa) I recognized you at once, Paoa. How wonderful to see you.

PAOA: And I to see you!

HIIAKA: Any news of Lohiau?

PAOA: None. Why don't we go to Kaua'i and search for his soul?

HIIAKA: I'm ready. Let's go now.

[They begin to go but stop when they see a giant cowrie shell vessel with ivory masts and white mats. This vessel could shrink to the size of a peanut or expand to the size of a huge ship.]

PAOA: There's only one person in it.

HIIAKA: Yes, I wonder who that is. Wait, he looks familiar. Oh, you know who that is?

PAOA: No.

HIIAKA: One of our relatives, the god Kanemilohai.

KANEMILOHAI: Hiiaka, I was just on my way to see you and to let you know I captured the soul of Lohiau between Kaua'i and Hawai'i. Once we got to Kilauea, I restored Lohiau to life.

PELE: (stands over Lohiau)

LOHIAU: (ready to appeal to her again for mercy)

PELE: (to Lohiau) Fear me no longer. After what I have done, I cannot expect your love. Find Hiiaka and give it to her. She loves you, and knows how to be kind to a mortal.

[Pele has vanished.]

KANEMILOHAI: Lohiau, you will find a cowrie shell vessel down on the beach. Sail it to Kaua'i where you will probably find Hiiaka and my friend Paoa. [Lohiau hesitates out of awe at Kanamilohai. He goes to the beach and finds a tiny cowrie shell.]

KANEMILOHAI: Be not afraid. It can expand or shrink to the size of your hand. The shell was not made in the sea or by human hands.

LOHIAU: It's only the size of a toy.

KANEMILOHAI: Put it in the edge of the sea.

[Lohiau does so.]

LOHIAU: I don't believe it. It is a huge vessel now.

KANEMILOHAI: I told you. Now I will confer upon you the power to enlarge or shrink this vessel.

[He does so.]

There, you now have the power. Now take this pink and pearl vessel, point your finger in the direction you wish to go, and it will go there.

[Lohiau points in the direction of Kaua'i but points too far north and lands at O'ahu.]

LOHIAU: I love the harbor here at Honolulu. Here I'll contract this vessel to the size of a limpet and secrete it in the niche in the rocks and head off to this village of Honolulu where I've heard Hiiaka and Paoa are visiting. And there is so much merriment and feasting going on. So that's what it is: the temporary residents of the alii-nui, high chiefs, kahunas, adventurers, surfers, and hula dancers from all parts of O'ahu. And tonight there is a feast in honor of Hiiaka and Omeo. (aside) I think I'll stay here and disguise myself and watch the festivities. If I announce myself, it would call attention to me and I would be accorded great honors befitting my rank. (aside) Look at all the torches, hundreds of them, and guests crowned with blossoms, having a feast from land and sea. And white-bearded bards chanting wild legends of the past such as Ohia and Lehua, Naupaka and Kaui as well as singers praising the hostess and her guests. Others have gone into the mansion to play the game of kilu. (aside) I'll go in to the mansion and watch the game of kilu. No one will recognize me with my royal yellow mantle turned inward and my long hair falling over my face and shoulders. They'll think I'm just another watching a kilu game. Not even those old chiefs will recognize me so intent are they on watching the kilu game. (aside) Oh, it's Hiiaka's turn.

HIIAKA: (sings) My tender love, Lohiau, my true love the hula dancer, my Prince of Kaua'i.

[People clap at the end of the song.]

LOHIAU: (sings) My true love, my wife Hiiaka, as constant as the waves at Puna...

[He brushes his hair back and turns his royal yellow mantle outward. The throng divided and he advanced toward Hiiaka. He is recognized at once as the Prince of Kaua'i. Hiiaka throws her arms around him as Paoa weeps with joy. Informed of the presence of such royalty, the throng vies to honor him in many ways and the feasting goes on long into the night. The next morning, Lohiau takes Hiiaka and Paoa to the beach.]

LOHIAU: (to Hiiaka and Paoa) I must get back to my people. I'll expand this shell barge made for me from Kanemilohai and we'll sail to Kaua'i. I must get back to my people. I know you understand.

HIIAKA: Certainly my prince.

PAOA: Of course. You are our prince, our sovereign chief. [Hiiaka soon returned to Hawai'i and effected a complete reconciliation with Pele. While Lohiau lived Hiiaka spent much of her time in Kaua'i. Hopoe was restored to life and Omeo was given an immortal form for what she had done and was thereafter a mediator between the volcanic deities.]

A Crude Awakening

a play in one act

Cast of Characters

BYRD: a student and friend of Geoff and Reed
GEOFF: a poet, friend, and fellow student
REED: another student and friend
T.C.:   Reed's father

Scene

Byrd's bedroom which is a bunkhouse, converted out of the original garage. It is next to the carport where Reed's father's well-used car is parked.

Time

The not-too-distant present.

Scene 1

Byrd, Geoff, and Reed in Reed's bunkhouse after midnight. The three friends are in an intense discussion. Reed is on his top bunk. Geoff is sprawled on the trundle bed. Byrd is seated in an office chair that rocks back toward a book case and chest of drawers.

REED: I don't know what to tell you, Byrd. I've heard so much of this before.
(a long pause as each takes another swallow of ice cold beer)

GEOFF: It sounds to me like you're getting the full brunt of Tanya's cock-and-bull games. She tells you one thing---oh I love you, Byrd, you're my one and only---
(he does this with a prolonged sigh while mimicking statues of lovesick Eros) and then turns around and she's with someone else without telling you. Like she did tonight. To me, man, that's a wakeup call. A rude one at that. So you come over here and drown your troubles in some brew.

BYRD: You don't seem to understand. I *do* love her.

REED: (piping in) You got it bad and that ain't good, as the song goes.

GEOFF: Then suffer, buddy. You gotta control your own destiny. She does this stuff and then when she wants you back, you go crawling back.

BYRD: I don't need your pontifications, Geoff. You should broaden your own empathy.

GEOFF: (who smirks then changes his tone) I'm just trying to tell you —

BYRD: (interrupting) You never liked her anyway. So it's no big deal for you.

GEOFF: (sighs deeply)

REED: Just keep in mind, Byrd, we just don't like to watch you, our friend, suffer at the hands of someone who keeps playing you. It's a pattern. You know she keeps flirting with Hunt.

GEOFF: (admonishingly) And that's who she was with tonight...

BYRD: Okay. Okay. She *was* with Hunt tonight.

GEOFF: Wouldn't you like to jack up his face? Punch him out? I would.

BYRD: Yeah. That would be worth it. But—

GEOFF: But what?

BYRD: I have to hear it from her.

GEOFF: Hear it from her? Her actions tonight speak volumes, man. Can't you see it?

BYRD: (glowers at Geoff) Shut up, Geoff. You're about as sensitive as...

GEOFF: (looks at Reed) I don't have to put up with this garbage.
(pleadingly at Reed) You try to help the guy...and he's not gonna listen...

BYRD: (scoffs at Geoff) Then leave, why don't you? (mocking and mimicking Geoff) That way you don't have to put up with such garbage!

GEOFF: (rises to go) I'm leaving. (shakes his fist at Byrd)

REED: (with his hand bids him stay. Geoff sits down again.)
The hour is late, you guys. I feel like I am mediating between a jester and a fool.

BYRD: That's inspiring. Thanks! You don't need to tell me who the fool is.
(He nods at Reed in Geoff's direction).

GEOFF: Yes, yes, yes. You don't need to tell us who the fool is, Reed. I'm looking right at him. (He glares at Byrd).

BYRD: And I am looking right at him.

REED: (conciliatory) Okay, okay. Fools can mirror each other. I can always play the joker.

GEOFF: We're all fools to spend our night, our get together, wasting it on a fool.

BYRD: (angry) Don't refer to Tanya that way.

GEOFF: (deliberately) I wasn't referring to Tanya.

BYRD: Go to hell, Geoff. You're about as sensitive as a—

REED: Jester. A court jester.

GEOFF: Reed, you're not helping anything.

REED: Okay, okay. (to Geoff) How can we help this guy who has a needle through his heart?

GEOFF: I say bid her adieu. Bon voyage. If she wants Hunt, so be it. I dated Tanya only one time…

BYRD: (interrupting) *You*? *You* dated her? You? When?

GEOFF: (tentatively) Oh, about a year or so ago.

BYRD: *You*? You dated her. (He pauses, smirks, takes another swallow of beer).

GEOFF: Yes. I did.

BYRD: This is quite a revelation. Do you like her?

GEOFF: Yes. She is nice. Very attractive…(after a pause)… but not for me.

BYRD: Why not? You could be wriggling in pain right now…as I speak. It could be you having to compete with Hunt. It could be you being lied to, being betrayed by her.

GEOFF: (glowering at him somewhat sarcastically) But it *isn't* me, is it now?

BYRD: (clenching his fist) I wouldn't say anything bad about her if *I* were you.

GEOFF: I'm not saying anything bad about her. (a long pause ensues; each of them drinks)

BYRD: (after a longer pause) So tell me---why, oh wise one, wasn't she for you?

GEOFF: I had fun at the dance with her. But you remember that guy…if I remember correctly, his name was Tondo, kind of an artistic guy who also wanted to be a building contractor…

BYRD: (almost eager) Oh, yeah. Didn't he want to build bridges?

GEOFF: I think so…I remember something like that. Well, he was at the dance.

BYRD: So what? Was he boring you with his desire to build bridges?

GEOFF: Well, in the course of the evening…she took a liking to Tondo. I remember when I went to get her a drink…I come back and she is dancing with him. All sequin-eyed, swept up into his cheek-to-cheek charms…she looked dazzled, in love.

BYRD: Bah! You're exaggerating!

68

GEOFF: No, I'm not. But it gets better…

BYRD: How?

GEOFF: I go over to her…to give her her drink…and you know what?

BYRD: She was out of the hoop…in a state of pure joy? Flew the coop?

GEOFF: Pretty much. And it didn't take long. Even I was shocked. Apparently Tondo wagged his finger and Tanya was right there. It hadn't even been more than five minutes and she was distracted.

BYRD: Maybe she just didn't like you.

GEOFF: And maybe, wise guy, she doesn't like you either. That's why Hunt is still in the game.

BYRD: (glares at Geoff and after a long pause) So what did you do?

GEOFF: I realized this was not something I wanted to be in. As much as I liked Tanya she struck me as a superficial opportunist. She had already begun playing me at a dance…on a first date no less! It took awhile, but I grew wise to her.

BYRD: But what did you do? Did you go and punch out Tondo?

GEOFF: No need to do that. I had no quarrel with him. My quarrel, if you can call it that, was with Tanya. She was the problem.

BYRD: (repeats) So what did you do about it?

GEOFF: Decided to pursue other interests. There were other women around like Carolina, Eva, Fiorella, Justine. I decided not to chase Tanya. But I could see how men would spend their time chasing her. Her beauty covers a multitude of lies.

REED: (offers) Bravo, Geoff, bravo. Now, Byrd, you need to do that, too.

GEOFF: Before it's too late.

BYRD: It's much too late for me. I'm hooked and that's that.

REED: (with sympathy) But you can get out of this…pain.

BYRD: You forget I love her. I really love her.

GEOFF: Then you will ride a roller coaster of pain and pleasure. One moment yes, one moment no. She's as fickle as Fortune.

REED: And Fortune doesn't mind flicking you off her tilt-a-whirl anytime there's a strain in the curve.

GEOFF: Amen, bro. Amen.

REED: So what are you going to do?

BYRD: (pauses) How do I know you're not just whitewashing her so we'll break up and you can have her all for yourself?

GEOFF: (in disbelief) Have you been listening? (to Reed) Can you believe this guy?

REED: (bewildered) I am astonished, Byrd. After all we've talked about tonight! Get your head out of your mistrust. We just happen to be your friends.

BYRD: But not all friends are true.

GEOFF: That's sometimes true. But I can't believe you would think such a thing of us.

REED: Believe me, Byrd, I wouldn't be a lounge lizard on this bed listening if I were not your friend. Wasn't it Aristotle who said a friend is a second self?

GEOFF: (confirming) Yes, I think you're right, Reed.

REED: Self-doubt and low self-esteem make for a drowning man.

BYRD: Oh, now you're analyzing me?

REED: (waves off an angry Geoff) No, no, we're not going to analyze anyone. We're just saying you are our friend. And we're both trying to help out. That's all. If you want to think that Geoff here is scheming on Tanya, that's your problem. He just told you what his experience was with Tanya. So get off your high horse!

BYRD: (conciliatory after a long pause and a long drink) Maybe you're right.

GEOFF: I like that. *Maybe* we're right. (looks at Reed and says sarcastically) Now that's a vote of confidence!

REED: Can't beat confidence. Not in this game. You gotta trust somebody. You can trust your true friends.

GEOFF: Going around doubting people, especially your friends, is not a bright idea.

BYRD: But you never mentioned you had ever dated Tanya. Why now?

GEOFF: Because it was not that important enough to even talk about. It was a momentary thing and I am glad I made the hard decision I made. But when I see my friend in the throes of this miserable situation, I thought it might be wise to tell you, seeing how it *is* relevant now. That's why I told you about it. About the dance and all.

REED: (gesturing to Byrd while looking at Geoff) It seems our friend here is...

GEOFF: A doubting Thomas. Like Reed said...you gotta trust somebody. We're all connected. I feel a special kinship with most poets. But not just poets. We're *all* connected. We may not want to acknowledge that. But we are.

(a long pause)

BYRD: (after awhile, thinking it over) I don't believe all this is really happening. I doubt myself sometimes.

REED: That's okay. That's okay. You know feelings like love can only aggravate and distort the situation. (after a long pause) A toast to friends. (Reed holds up his mug; Geoff is slow to toast; Byrd is even slower but finally they toast each other and drink)

GEOFF: Sometimes only misery allies with wishful thinking.

REED: Amen, bro.

GEOFF: So we're back to the original question. What are you going to do?

BYRD: I don't know. I really don't. If I could only kill these feelings...

REED: There's nothing wrong with your feelings; it's just that it is hard to live your life, go to school, do your job with her on your mind.

BYRD: (nods)

GEOFF: There's no telling what she and Hunt are up to...without you knowing about it. They may be sleeping together...

BYRD: (suddenly) I don't want to talk about...you hear me, Geoff! I don't want to talk about it.

GEOFF: (holding his hands up) Whoa! No harm meant. Just trying to face facts. That's the hard part.

BYRD: I don't want to talk about the facts. I am too miserable. I'm being pulled apart inside like horses galloping in all directions, drawn and quartered, like my heart is being diced by a thousand knives. I'm bleeding inside. Can't you see that?

GEOFF: (holding his head down, shaking it) I do now. Sorry. I've said enough. I meant no harm. None at all.

REED: (to Byrd) He didn't mean it. Take it easy. Let's not do any finger pointing now. You can go on and tell us anything you want. Or not say anything.

GEOFF: (sincerely) I didn't want to add any pain. Goodness knows...

BYRD: (in earnest) Well, you did....you did.

REED: (after a pause) I propose another toast.

GEOFF: To...recovering...from pain. Finding love that overcomes love.

BYRD: (somewhat puzzled) I don't know what all that means. Sounds good. I'll drink to that.

GEOFF: Me too. (they all toast)

REED: (continues) Anyway, we're with you, buddy. Anything we can do. Just let us know.

BYRD: (nods with gratitude) Thanks.
(after a pause) Well, I should be going.

GEOFF: (alarmed) Going? In your condition? We're all on a buzz by now.

REED: I agree. I'm higher than Mount Everest. Just stay the night. Keeps you off the road. That's all you need...to crash into a tree or telephone pole. You can sleep on the trundle bed. Geoff and I can take the bunk beds. My folks won't mind.
(Reed rolls out the trundle bed for Byrd who goes outside. A pause.)

GEOFF: Where is Byrd?

REED: Relieving himself in the night.

GEOFF: I hope he can find his way back.

REED: He will. Here's a pillow for your bunk. You already have a couple of blankets.
(suddenly Byrd leans in the door)

72

BYRD: Hey, you guys. Check out the eyes over there!

GEOFF: (hops off the top bunk) What's going on?

BYRD: Over there. By the fish pond. See those yellow-green eyes?

REED: (quickly follows Geoff) Oh, don't worry about that. It's just a raccoon. Let me get a flashlight.
(he goes outside; standing next to Byrd, he turns on the flashlight)

REED: See, he's gone. They're swift and cunning.
(goes to the other side of a fish pond)
Got one of our koi. They leave part of the fish even if I don't get out here to scare them away. They love salmon heads. That's the only way I can trap them. I usually chase 'em over that fence. But not tonight. I'm a little weighed down with brew. Let's go, Byrd. It's been a long night.
(once inside the bunk house, he looks at Geoff)
He's gone. They really move. I've seen them go over a seven foot fence like it's nothing. Poof! Faster than a cheetah.

GEOFF: You have raccoons all the time?

REED: There's a nest on the hill behind the house. They're abundant believe me.

GEOFF: Must be a lot of strange sounds in the night out here. But I live in town and I hear sounds all night. Fire engines. Ambulances. Nightclubs. Cars engines revving up. But you get used to it. I can sleep through most things.

REED: That's good. Because there are lots of strange sounds around here, too. Our peacocks sometimes get in different trees and decide they want to have a little chat. It's kind of a blood-curdling cry. Like a distress signal.

GEOFF: Yeah. I've heard peacocks before. Wicked. You never forget the cry of a peacock.

REED: I'm glad you're used to them because we definitely have them out here in the country.

BYRD: As you know, Reed, I can sleep through anything. Once I'm in a deep sleep, I'm like a rock.

REED: I agree. You *are* a sound sleeper, Byrd. Many a fishing trip. (after a pause) Well, let's get some sleep. (Reed turns out the light)

Scene 2

A couple of hours later: the bunk house where Reed and Byrd have gone to sleep. Geoff wakes up.

GEOFF: (awake) Where am I? (He looks at his watch in the faint light and whispers) Almost five-thirty.

GEOFF: What is that? (he reaches up and shakes Reed)

GEOFF: (whispers) Hey Reed. Reed. Wake up.

REED: Wha—What? (a pause) What's going on? (begins looking for the clock) What on earth? What time is it?

GEOFF: Five-thirty.

REED: (they both listen to Byrd snoring)

GEOFF: (to Reed) How can you sleep with this going on?

REED: That's right. You haven't been camping with all of us. It's a common reaction.

GEOFF: I bet it is. I was having a nightmare. I thought we were being invaded! (puts his head in his hands) You know what that sounds like? B-52s on a bombing mission!

REED: (chuckles low) I gotta admit. If you're not used to Byrd's snoring, it can be a bit traumatic.

GEOFF: (frowning) A bit? A bit traumatic? I couldn't figure out what was happening. No one snores like this. It's obscene.

REED: (with a twinkle in his eye) There are positive things about it. When we go camping, even the grizzlies stay away. Not to mention the deer.

GEOFF: That's nice to know. I'll remember not to go camping with you all, especially when Byrd is invited. I just wasn't prepared for this. For the first couple hours I seem to have been dead to the world. But then…then I heard this steady, loud, uncouth, snoring. At first I thought it was machine gun fire. Or a hydraulic jack. Truly unbelievable.

74

REED: (agreeing) It *is* loud. No question about that.

GEOFF: (quizzically) Tell me, have you ever been able to go back to sleep after his snoring?

REED: Depends on how tired I am. After awhile, you get used to it. If you've never heard it before — like you — it has to be traumatic. (Just then Byrd snorts for a moment then resumes snoring)

GEOFF: For a moment there I thought he might wake up. Instead, he sounded like a wild boar. I was ready to call in the Great Danes.

REED: No, he doesn't wake up. Last summer we all went camping with Damian and Kristof. They asked the same question. No, he really doesn't. Believe me, it is rare that he wakes up. He just sleeps like a worn out dog. Especially after all the beer he's had. You'd think he's been at the Oktoberfest in Munich.

GEOFF: So what do you do?

REED: Try to get some sleep.

GEOFF: Good luck. (Just then Reed's dad's rooster crows)

GEOFF: Good God! What's that?

REED: Our rooster. Our champion rooster.

GEOFF: Every morning he does this?

REED: Like clockwork. He's our alarm clock.

GEOFF: You don't get up at this hour, do you?

REED: I usually sleep right through it.

GEOFF: We don't have to worry about Byrd sleeping through it. His snoring hasn't missed a beat. (they pause to listen to Byrd's steady, loud snoring)

GEOFF: If you sleep right through it, why do you say your rooster is an alarm clock?

REED: Oh, because my dad gets up about the same time.

GEOFF: He's up now? This early?

REED: Sure. He has probably already fed the chickens, geese, and ducks.

GEOFF: Why does he get up so early?

REED: He loves to watch the sunrise. (after a pause) He also goes into the garden and cuts the corn before the sugar goes back down into the stalk. See the sugar rises during the night and then goes

75

back down into the ground in the morning. The idea is to cut the stalk so that the sugar remains in the ears of corn. That makes the corn much sweeter. Then he takes our old car and drives into town to get things we need, you know, such as feed or maybe fertilizer for the yard.

(they hear a gate close)

REED: He's up already. Crack of dawn. (after a pause)

GEOFF: Why does Byrd call your dad "The Grey Ghost"?

REED: He likes to wear the same gray sweatshirt in the yard. My mom doesn't like him to though. But it *is* his favorite.

GEOFF: What does *she* want him to wear?

REED: Shoes and pants that don't have holes in them. A different sweatshirt. She says it makes him look like he can't afford decent clothes. But he told me he just likes that particular sweatshirt. That's how he got the nickname "Grey Ghost."

GEOFF: Why does he wear pants and shoes with holes in them?

REED: Well, probably because he wears a suit all day at work. I imagine it feels good to get out of that garb and into something more loosey goosey.

(they hear geese honking and ducks quacking)

REED: Sure. (he goes to the window)

GEOFF: Are those the geese?

REED: It's hard to tell with Byrd snoring But yeah. Come over here and I'll show you.

(Geoff goes to the window)

REED: See. They follow my dad to where he feeds them. See that big gander over there whose trying to peck the other geese in the pecking order?

GEOFF: The big gray one with the orange beak?

REED: Yes, that's right. That's Senator Stone, our prize gander. He took first prize in last year's town and country fair.

GEOFF: (almost surprised) He *is* a big gander. I didn't know they were that big.

REED: (confirming) Oh, he's a thoroughbred Toulouse. Originated in France. They are superb watchdogs.

76

Sometimes Byrd arrives and as soon as he's on the property, they start honking. Geese are wonderful watchdogs.

GEOFF: Just think even their honking has not disturbed Byrd at all. He's snoring away, sawing wood with the best of them.

REED: You'd think he would be up early since he was so upset last night.

GEOFF: I think the beer put him out for quite some time.

REED: Yeah. He should sleep for quite awhile.

GEOFF: What about us?

REED: What *about* us?

GEOFF: When will *we* get some sleep?

REED: Some time later today.

(just then they hear a car door slam shut)

REED: Uh, oh. This should be interesting. My dad just got into his car.

GEOFF: In the carport?

REED: (nods)

GEOFF: How far away is it?

REED: Maybe ten feet.

GEOFF: You think it will wake up Byrd?

REED: It wakes me up. I don't know about him.

(the sound of a Reed's dad's trying to start the car begins; it goes on for about ten seconds)

GEOFF: I'm glad I didn't try to go back to sleep. That would wake me up, too.

REED: Just as well. (the car tries to start again; this time it goes on for about thirty seconds)

GEOFF: If he keeps that up, it'll flood the engine.

REED: Not our car. It specializes in *not* being flooded.

GEOFF: What do you mean?

REED: It just doesn't flood. It keeps on grinding.

(the car is heard trying to start again, this time for about twenty seconds)

GEOFF: That grinding noise alone would wake up the dead!

REED: That's why I don't get a whole lot of sleep around here in the morning. If our rooster doesn't wake you up, my dad's car will. (the sound of Reed's dad trying to star the car begins again, this time for twenty more seconds)

GEOFF: Isn't he's going to ruin the transmission?

REED: No, not that car. It has a most unusual engine.

GEOFF: It sure does! It's bound to ruin the engine.

REED: I thought so too. That's was a few years ago. It seems to thrive on taking a long time to get started. (the car tries starting again, this time for thirty seconds)

GEOFF: You've got to be kidding. How does this engine do it? It just keeps on grinding.

REED: I don't know.

GEOFF: I would've thought not only would the engine flood, but the transmission would be shot by now.

REED: Not this engine.

(the car tries starting again, this time even longer)

GEOFF: (reaches down and touches Reed's arm) Uh, oh, I just heard a gap in the snoring.

REED: (surprised) You're right.

(they look across the room to the trundle bed)

GEOFF: (bewildered, amazed) How could anyone sleep through all this?

REED: (indicating Byrd) So far he has.

(Reed's dad keeps trying to start the car engine)

GEOFF: What kind of engine is in that car?

REED: One straight out of hell. I guarantee it.

GEOFF: You would think that by now---

(just then Byrd actually stirs)

REED: I think it's finally getting to him. Even Byrd.

GEOFF: Even Byrd after several beers.

(the car tries starting again, this time for another thirty seconds)

REED: (whispers urgently) Shhhhhhhhhhhhhh.

BYRD: (groggy and begins to wake up) What's going on? (he looks around as if he is on another planet) What is that grinding noise? that endless grinding noise? (puts his head in his hand as though his hangover is severe)What is that insane grinding? It's driving me crazy! I'm losing it! (he goes to the window and with one arm in a sweeping motion pushes up the Venetian blinds and stares out the window) Tanya! I don't believe it. You witch! Is this some kind of torture test? I'm being haunted by that woman!

REED: (puzzled, looks at Geoff) Tanya?! No, it's my dad's car. He does that in the morning. It just takes awhile to get the car started.

BYRD: I swear it's Tanya! (he rubs his eyes) It is!

REED: It is *not* Tanya!

BYRD: Yes, it is!

REED: (with a skeptical look) No, it is not. Look again. It's my dad.

GEOFF: It's his dad, Byrd. The Grey Ghost.

BYRD: It's Tanya.

REED: (to Geoff) Let's go take a look. (they go to the window)

GEOFF: It *is* Tanya! (with a wink)

REED: (to Geoff) You too? (looks out the window) It's my dad. He sure doesn't look like Tanya, believe me. (looks puzzled at both Byrd and Geoff)
What's got into you two?

BYRD: I told you. It's Tanya!

GEOFF: Really, it is, Reed. Byrd's not lying. Take another look!

REED: I don't believe you two! (just then the car starts)

GEOFF: I don't believe it. The car started. Listen to that engine hum!

BYRD: It *is* incredible. It should have died long ago. That grinding sound just about---

REED: Let me go talk to my dad. We can straighten this out right away. Let me get my moccasins on...and talk to him before he leaves. (goes out the door)

BYRD: This should tell the tale. Wait till he gets an earful from Tanya.

GEOFF: She can really give an earful. Let's watch.

BYRD: Let's keep an eye on Reed. He just may be in denial. Know what I mean?

GEOFF: I sure do. And that's unusual for Reed. (Reed goes up to the car)

REED: Hi, Dad.

T.C.: (smiles) What is it, son?

REED: Oh, I was wondering---

T.C.: Wondering what?

REED: Are you going into town?

T.C.: Well, I'm on my way to get a few things.

REED: Could you pick up a pack of gum for me?

T.C.: Sure, what kind?

REED: Spearmint would be good.

T.C.: Sure. Be glad to. (after a moment)
I see some of your friends are here. (looks at the other car in the driveway)

REED: We talked late into the night.

T.C.: Ah, I see. (takes a puff on his cigarette) Maybe they can get some sleep after I leave.

REED: I'm sure they'll get some later. They were sure you were someone else.

T.C.: Me?

REED: Yeah. Byrd's having girl problems.

T.C.: (smiles knowingly) A common problem at your age. Actually, a common problem at any age, come to think of it. He'll get over it. In time, he'll get over it. Someday, as I told you awhile back, you can look back and laugh at all the hopes, pain, dreams and fireworks.

REED: Yeah. I remember. Thanks. See you in awhile. And thanks...for the gum, too.

T.C.: You're welcome. See you in awhile. (at that point he backs the car out of the driveway)

REED: (returns to his room where Byrd and Geoff are talking low to one another) Sorry, guys, that was my dad. He's bringing me some gum. I had to make up something, some reason I was out there talking to him at this hour.

GEOFF: You convinced me. I must have been seeing things.

BYRD: I stand by my original vision. It was Tanya. That witch!

REED: My dad gave me some advice not too long ago.

BYRD: Oh, yeah. And what was that?

REED: That you'll get over it. And move where you're supposed to be going. Meet the one you're supposed to meet.

BYRD: Not bad for the Grey Ghost. But I tell you, it was Tanya at the wheel.

REED: Our minds can be sleight of hands, jugglers between rocks and wishes. Some cherish their illusions and get attached to them.

BYRD: I'm not trying to play tricks on myself, Reed. I tell you I saw her at the wheel.

REED: Well, Geoff, we have a lot of work to do with our friend Byrd here. Much to do.

GEOFF: Yes, we do. Cleaning the avenues of perception, for starters. (Byrd smiles receptively)

REED: Being able to see beyond sight. That's a fine goal.

GEOFF: And a painful one. We've been through this before. And we'll help you get through this.

REED: Indeed. We will.

The Fortune Telling Parrot

Cast of Characters

JIN	teacher and the owner of Lam, his pet parrot
UNA	Jin's live-in girlfriend
LAM	the Parrot, one of whose talents is fortune telling
POLO	banker and lover of Una
BRUNO	a businessman and lover of Una
TV Voices:	chief chef Breton and his assistants, Jan, Margarita
Moira	a friend of Jin
Dr. Jack	a professor of history
Chance	Una look alike who portrays Fortune

Scene

Jin's apartment in the city.

Time

2003

ACT I

Scene 1

SETTING: Jin's apartment.
AT RISE: Jin and Una are in a passionate embrace on the couch. The phone rings.

JIN: Who could that be…at this hour? (He goes to the phone and answers). Hello. (pause) Hello. (He hangs up the phone and looks at the clock) It's after one in the morning. The person hung up.

UNA: Oh, don't worry about it. Probably a wrong number. Now let's get back to where we were.

LAM: Probably a wrong number. Ha, ha, ha, ha.

UNA: (frowns) Go back to sleep, Lam. Way past your bedtime.

LAM: Bedtime, bedtime. Ha, ha, ha, ha.

JIN: (admonishing) Goodnight, Lam. (to Una) Don't get him started. He'll keep us up all night long with his stories.

UNA: Good idea.

JIN: I should get some sleep. Big day tomorrow. That field trip is gonna make us late. I won't be home until six or six-thirty.

UNA: I'll miss you, dear. (more serious) Yes, why don't we get some sleep.

JIN: Let's do. (they fold back the covers, turn off the light, and go to sleep) Goodnight, my love.

UNA: Goodnight, dear. I hope you have a sound night's sleep. There's nothing like sleep to calm the heart and mind at the end of the day.

JIN: It does feel relaxing. It does. Well, goodnight, my love.

UNA: May sweet dreams soothe away the cares of day. Goodnight, love.

JIN: You have such a nice way of putting it, Una. You really do.

Scene 2

Jin has left for work. Una is reading a women's magazine on the couch. Lam tilts his head while eating nuts. The phone rings.

UNA: (picks up the phone) Hello. Yes, he does. But only on the weekends. Down by Lillebonne Park. It's only a dollar. Oh, around 10 o'clock. Yes on the west side. You can't miss him. He sets up a table and then if you want to know your fortune, you simply buy a ticket...Sure, I go too. Where do the fortunes come from? Why, that's a trade secret. Just come down to the park...and you'll see. No, I don't give out cell phone numbers. Sorry.
(hangs up the phone)

LAM: (mimics a phone ringing) R-r-r-r-r-r-r-r-r-ing. R-r-r-r-r-r-r-r-r-ing.

UNA: Quiet, Lam! Stop it! (the parrot stops and tilts its head) Good boy! (she sits down and begins again reading her magazine when the phone rings) Oh, hi. Sure. I'm alone...You shouldn't say such things, Polo. Somebody could be listening. Sure. I guess you could. I'd love to see you. Don't let anybody see you. No, he won't be back till late. You can come by. See you in a few. She hangs up and goes into the bathroom; comes back with a makeup kit, combs her hair, and puts on makeup)

Scene 3

Polo pays a visit; a somewhat tall, muscular, fellow with wavy black hair and cordial smile. Una and Polo are in a loving embrace on the bed.

UNA: (almost breathless) I love you, too, Polo. It has been too long. Two whole nights without you. But we must be discreet, you know. I can let you know when the time is ripe. There's nobody here during the day. Oh, Polo, I do love you so.

POLO: (in earnest) Two whole nights is way too long. A thousand kisses would not be enough. More I could give, my love Una. I'll be discreet. This is the best time for me, too. I do love you, Una. (after several more kisses)

POLO: You don't have to stay here. Come live with me. I want to see you every night when I get home.

UNA: (smiles at first, then vaguely frowns) I don't know, Polo. You have a nice place...but your mom comes over to see you almost every day. And she doesn't like me. She has made that quite clear on more than one occasion.

POLO: (almost defensive) She's always that way. There is one girl she has ever liked...and she got married two years ago. She'll just have to get used to the idea that—
(just then the doorbell rings)

UNA: (to Polo in a whisper) Shhhhhhshhhhhshhhh.
(there is a long pause)
(the doorbell rings again)

POLO: (whispers) Who could that be?

UNA: (shakes her head; another pause; the sound of a paper being pushed under the door can be heard) It might be better...if you leave. This doesn't happen during the day. At least while I am here.

POLO: (determined) I shall stay with my love. I'll confront whoever's there. I'll do battle if I have to.

UNA: (quite concerned) This is not the time, Polo. You're a dear to say that. But this is no time for heroics. It's a time for discretion.

LAM: (injects) Most times are.

POLO: (resigned) So, I'll go. I'll call you.

UNA: (calculating) No, no. Let me call you. This afternoon.
(they head for the door; Polo notices the paper under the door and picks it up and reads it)

POLO: (with a stunned look) Do you know someone named Bruno?

UNA: (with shock, replies tentatively) Why...yes. Yes.

POLO: (with a look that would dismantle a wild boar) A gaucho....named Bruno? A gaucho? A *gaucho*?

UNA: (defensively) He's just a friend. I have many friends.

POLO: (looks at her skeptically) I see. It *is* nice to have so many friends. Is this one from Argentina?

UNA: (in a matter of fact tone) Yes, I believe he hails from there...originally. Why, what did he say?

POLO: (disgusted) He didn't have the decency to close it so even the mail carrier could've read it!

UNA: Well, what did he say?
(Polo hands her the note)
"You will soon be in the arms of someone who loves you. Te amo, Bruno the Gaucho."
(she folds the note and puts it in her purse)

POLO: (with a skeptical tone) Sounds like he's in the business of telling fortunes. Too bad he doesn't go back to the Pampas, instead of being pompous.

UNA: (almost defensive) He just likes to say such things.

POLO: (skeptical) Kind of like the way I say "I love you"...to you?

UNA: (rationalizing) Nothing like that. (assuringly) You have nothing to worry about.

POLO: I had better go. Give me a call when you have a chance.
(leaves) (after a long pause)

UNA: (stands like someone who has been indecently exposed) Of all the times. Bruno shows up.

LAM: But you *do* have a propensity for gauchos, madame.

UNA: (fiercely) Shut up, Lam! I'm putting the cover back over your cage. You talk too much! (puts cover over Lam's cage)

Scene 4

Jin comes home. Una watches TV. Lam is silent.

JIN: Hey, how's my honey? (Una helps him with his briefcase)

UNA: I'm okay. How was your day?

JIN: Fine. Got a lot done. Students were okay. Learned some things. The usual.

(after a pause) I got a call today. A curious call.

UNA: You did? Anything important?

JIN: Just a complaint.

UNA: A complaint? About what?

JIN: You know the routine.

UNA: What routine?

JIN: (looks at the mail on the chest of drawers) Oh... just a disgruntled guy.

UNA: A guy? (she tries to look unconcerned but cannot hide her concern)

JIN: (goes to Lam's cage and talks to the parrot) Oh, about a fortune he got...from Lam here. It seems Lam did not give him the fortune he was expecting.

UNA: Well, you know Lam. He can be full of surprises.

JIN: He's been that way since he was just a baby parrot when I took him off the hands of the man down by the docks.

UNA: Yes, he can be full of surprises. So what was wrong with the fortune?

JIN: I don't know what he was expecting but he was not expecting this particular one.

UNA: Well, tell me about it. You've got me curious.

JIN: (begins changing channels with the TV remote) Oh, the fortune was about---oh, wonderful. A polo match. I haven't seen one of those since the Gatsby Affair over in Santa Rosa. I love polo. One of my favorite sports.

UNA: (with hesitation) I love Polo, too. It's a sublime sport.

LAM: (with gusto) I love you, Polo.

JIN: See, even Lam loves a good sport, too. He's a brilliant bird. Not many parrots have the kind of knowledge he does. Not many parrots are trained in philosophy.

UNA: That's for sure. I don't understand all that.

JIN: You know, even when he was a tiny bird, he always struck me as brighter than usual. (to Lam) We love you, too, Lam.

UNA: (looking disgusted as well as apprehensive) Well, sometimes he can be a… good bird. At other times, he can be…(trying to find the right word) ugh…a dirty bird, I mean loud.

JIN: You know how parrots are.

UNA: Not really. Except they can be full of surprises. (goes to the kitchen and brings back a plate of chips and some drinks)

JIN: They certainly can be. (listens to the polo match) Yeah, they were here last year. The Dan Bruno Gauchos.

UNA: (with concern) Oh, yes. They were here last year.

LAM: A gaucho named Bruno. Ha, ha, ha, ha.

JIN: No, Lam. The Dan Bruno Gauchos.

LAM: A gaucho named Bruno.

JIN: (with pride) You know, I think that bird has a mind of his own. (they continue to watch the polo match) Can you believe that hit? What a horse! Look how quickly it can turn! On a dime even!

UNA: (eager to change the subject) It shows a lot of riding, a lot of hard, dedicated riding.

JIN: Those horses are special. Here, you want another drink?

UNA: Yes, but I'll get it. (she goes to the kitchen) You want some more chips?

JIN: Sure. And could you get me some napkins. It's getting kinda messy in here. Oh, what a great swing!

UNA: (brings in another drink and napkins) Here you go. I like the Santa Rosa Polo Club. But they just might lose…

JIN: (nods) The Gauchos are good. Look how they command their horses! How they wheel about!

LAM: Ha, ha, ha, ha, ha. A gaucho named Bruno.

JIN: No, Lam. The Dan Bruno Gauchos. You got it all wrong. The team is the Dan Bruno Gauchos. Not a gaucho named Bruno.

UNA: (with concern) You're right, Jin. He does have a mind of his own.

Scene 5

A few days later at Lillebonne Park Jin and Lam are at their booth. Polo, a banker, is next in line.

POLO: I was the one who emailed you. I—
JIN: Ah, yes. You did not like your fortune. What was the problem again?
POLO: I did not like the fortune because it is not true. Here's what it said: "You and your wife will live happily together." (eyes the parrot who is eyeing him)
JIN: (surprised) That's a lovely fortune. Most people would like that! What is the problem with it?
POLO: (eyeing the parrot again) First, I am not even married.
JIN: Maybe it applies to your life in the future. You may be married before you know it.
LAM: (almost gleeful) He, he, he. You may be married *before* you know it!
POLO: Does your parrot always repeat stuff?
JIN: Sometimes. Sometimes he does…but not always. (to Lam) Hush, Lam. No commentary.
LAM: (looks painfully sad for a moment)
POLO: It is just not true. But, in addition, the rest of the fortune…I do not understand.
JIN: What part was that?
POLO: The part that reads: "It will take several lifetimes to discover the meaning of Being."
JIN: Oh, don't worry about that part of the fortune. My parrot does philosophize now and then. He's had some training in philosophy. I wouldn't take that part of the fortune seriously.
POLO: And what about these numbers? 0-18-12-6-9?
JIN: Oh, those are if you play the lottery. It's just a number combination that might just win… although you never know until you play.
POLO: I see. But there's no guarantee they will win the lottery. It's just a guess at best.

JIN: That's true. But you haven't tried them yet, have you?

POLO: (skeptical) No, I don't think they're the magic numbers. I doubt if you think they're the magic numbers.

JIN: You never know until you try.

POLO: And if you're wrong. Do I get my money back?

JIN: Since you are so upset, sure. You can have your money back.

POLO: They I'll go try them. (He leaves as the next customer in line pays to have her fortune read.)

JIN: Hello, Moira. I remember Moira because it is the word representing the Fates in Greek myth.

MOIRA: Oh, remember, you can call me by my nickname, Toots.

JIN: Thanks, Toots. (she eyes Lam)

MOIRA: (she continues to eye the parrot) How is Lam doin'? Seems as perky as ever.

JIN: He's doing fine. People seem to like their fortunes.

MOIRA: He's a smart bird. But, you know…although I like to get my fortune every time you're here, I don't take them that seriously. I just figure, what is to come, will be. So I don't fret about it.

JIN: You mean you pay good money for this…but you don't take it that seriously?

MOIRA: I just go and have a high ball, have a few laughs, and don't take it too seriously.

JIN: Well, there are some who take this fortune business so seriously, they get quite upset if they don't get what they want…or hear what they want to hear.

MOIRA: What they need is a good highball. That'll help wash their fortunes, both good and bad, away!

JIN: If it were only that simple, Toots! If it only were that simple! You want your fortune today?

MOIRA: I wouldn't miss it for the world! (eyeing Lam) My fate is in your hands, you silly bird!

LAM: (Lam squawks as if in response) He, he, heh, heh, he, he.

JIN: Here you go, Lam. She's paid for her ticket. (They watch as Lam selects with his beak from a row of fortunes).

LAM: There you go, Toots! Enjoy it! Tell 'em Lam lays it on thick! He, he, heh, heh, he, he.

MOIRA: We'll see what little Lam has brought to one of his most faithful and frequent customers. (She opens the card and reads it) "Someone influential will soon enter your life." Oh, brother, I've got that one before. No one influential has entered my life, except maybe the bartender at the Iron Horse Inn. I feel gypped. But that's okay, I feel gypped most of the time.

JIN: (puzzled) You can have your money back, Toots.

MOIRA: Don't worry about a thing. It's just the process of it all. And a way to support my friend and his lovely parrot, our little Lam.

JIN: No, seriously. You *can* have your money back.

MOIRA: Tut, tut, Jin. As I said before, I really don't take it seriously.

JIN: Well, what about the other parts of the fortune?

MOIRA: That's right. Lam here usually makes some kind of observation. Let's see...oh here it is. This is what it says: "Time's gravity is as curved as space is." That's good to know. Then I can know which way I should be walking after a couple of highballs!

JIN: (grinning) That should be of some practical value!

MOIRA: You bet. Of course. I wouldn't leave the planet without it.

JIN: See you later, Moira, I mean Toots! (Moira leaves the line as another customer steps up)

(Lights Fade)

ACT II

Scene 1

A day in the following week. Jin is at work. Una is watching a cooking show on TV while looking at a fashion magazine.

TV: Welcome to yet again another segment of *Bubbling with Bruno*. Today, our chef, Bruno Bréton, is going to give us some tips on how to make a delicious chicken with rice dish called in Spanish, appropriately enough, Arroz con Pollo. We also have with us two of his brilliant students at the Keggersdude Academy of the Culinary Arts, Margarita Soledad and Jan Ming Tao.

UNA: Hmmmmm. Maybe I can try this recipe. I know Bruno would like it. Maybe Jin would like it too.

LAM: Ha, ha, ha, heh, heh, Arroz con Polo, heh, heh, heh.

UNA: Stop squawking, Lam. I'm trying to listen to this show.

(she stops reading the fashion magazine and gets paper and pencil and listens)

BRETON: You get all the ingredients for Arroz con Pollo.

LAM: Ha, ha, heh: Arroz con Polo.

UNA: No, Lam. Stop squawking. It's pollo, not polo. It's Spanish.

MARGARITA: Besides chicken and rice you will need: lemon, garlic, onion, oregano, ham, tomato, green olives…(she motions to Jan to complete the ingredients)

JAN: and pimentos, capers, saffron, peas, and light beer.

BRETON: Thank you, ladies. Now for a delightful edition of Arroz con Pollo —

LAM: Heh, ha, ha. Arroz con Polo. Polo with chef Bruno!

UNA: Quiet! Stop talking, Lam. I'm trying to get this recipe.

LAM: A recipe from Chef Bruno who cooks polo.

UNA: (she goes to his cage and puts a cover over it) There! If you don't shut up, I'll cook your goose!

LAM: But I'm not a goose!
UNA: You will be! Now stuff it, if you know what's good for you!
(she turns her attention back to the TV)
JAN: Make sure the garlic is minced. Next, chop the onions, tomatoes, and ham.
MARGARITA: Oh, also make sure...you have half a bunch of cilantro which should be chopped.
BRETON: And, as for the lemon...lime can also be used. Make sure it is in juice form. Not sliced lemon or lime. Just juice.
LAM: Just juice it!
UNA: I'm warning you. Shut up! It's time for you to go on the lam, Lam. (she turns her attention back to the show)
Lam: I know when I'm tempting fortune. I'm going on the lam.
(she turns her attention back to the TV)
BRETON: The next thing to be done is to begin the marination. Take the chicken and garlic, the olive oil and lemon juice. Add some salt and pepper.
(he does this as Una is writing all of this down)
JAN: Once that is done pat the pieces of chicken dry. Then sauté them in small batches. Once that's done, put them on a platter.
UNA: So they should be sautéed...(just then the phone rings)
Wouldn't you know it. Right in the middle of the recipe. It looks like simmer after the pieces of chicken are sautéed...
(the phone rings again and again)
LAM: (mimics the phone) R-r-r-r-r-r-r-r-r-r-r-ing.
UNA: Quiet, Lam! (answers the phone)
Ah, hello Bruno! How wonderful to hear from you!
BRUNO: I have to see you, Una. It has been too long!
UNA: Well, I guess you can come over. But you have to be discreet about it. We have some nosy neighbors.
BRUNO: Don't worry about a thing. Discretion is my hallmark. I'll be there at 12:30.

UNA: (hangs up) Okay, I'd better get ready. That gives me just over an hour. (she turns up the TV volume) Let me jot down what I can to get the recipe right.

BRETON: So, to sum it all up, after the sauté phase of the onion, pepper, and garlic, you stir in the rice and sauté about one to two minutes and do the same with the ham.

JAN: Then all that is left is to put the chicken pieces back in, cover the pot, and simmer on low heat for about, let's say, thirty minutes.

MARGARITA: The finishing touch is to remove from the heat and let it rest, covered for about, say, ten minutes. Then add the cilantro, toss all the ingredients gently with a fork, and serve it up.

BRETON: And, just likes that, ladies and gentlemen, you have a Spanish dish delighted in by Puerto Rico and the Caribbean and so many other places. For now, that is today's recipe, Arroz con Pollo, for your eating pleasure. I'm Chef Bruno Breton saying "bon appetite" from all of us here, including these eminent chefs-to-be, Margarita Soledad and Jan Ming Tao, at *Bubbling with Bruno*.

UNA: Now for the makeover. (she exits into another room to freshen up)

Scene 2

Later, Una and Bruno are making out. Lam is quiet.

UNA: So glad you could make it, Bruno.

BRUNO: It has been torture to be without you. You know my love.

UNA: And you know mine.

BRUNO: I do. I do. (they kiss again) I love loving you. You are the bright spot in my day. I get bored at work. Signing papers, loan agreements. But then I think of you…and it all falls away.

UNA: (noticeably touched) Oh, Bruno, you are such a love. (after a pause) You know, I have never known a gaucho before.

BRUNO: Ah, that was a few years back. It was fun but also hard work. I prefer being in the business of business to that kind of life. I certainly prefer love to the banking life.

UNA: A gaucho's life. It all seems so...exotic.

BRUNO: Things seem exotic...especially from a distance. Especially the hard work in the life of a gaucho.

UNA: I can understand.

BRUNO: (after a pause) I prefer to see you here. Meeting all those times at the hotel got to be rather risqué. So just you and your boyfriend live here.

UNA: Well, my boyfriend and his pet parrot.

BRUNO: You own a parrot?

UNA: I don't but he does.

BRUNO: The parrot lives here?

UNA: Why, yes.

BRUNO: Here in your place?

UNA: Sure.

BRUNO: Where?

UNA: In that little corner of the next room.

BRUNO: Could I see your parrot?

UNA: (with a sour grimace) I thought you wanted to see me. We don't have much time. Jin will be home in just a little while.

BRUNO: You are right. Maybe another time. (they kiss)

UNA: No, you can see our parrot. One girl friend from Georgia used to call him Honey Lam. But his name is just Lam. (They get up and go to a corner of the next room. Una takes off the cage cover)

BRUNO: (startled) A handsome parrot. I've always been partial to blue-crown conures. A handsome parrot!

UNA: (matter of factly) No question about that.

BRUNO: (curious) So handsome but covered up. (Lam moves away from both of them in his cage)

UNA: He talks a lot. I was trying to copy down a recipe and he kept talking. So, one way to keep him quiet is to cover up his cage.

BRUNO: (curious) He *is* a handsome parrot. And he looks so familiar. Hmmm.

UNA: (gestures as if she has to go) You can visit with Lam. I'll be back in just a few.

(She goes into another room)

BRUNO: (moves closer to the cage) You want to know a little secret?

(recites) "There once was a gaucho named Bruno (that's me) who said:

'There's one thing I do know:
That Lola is fine,
And Carmen divine,
But Una is numero uno.'"

(Lam listens intently.)

And don't you forget that, Señor Lam. Such nice gray and red feathers you have. You *do* look familiar. But I bet you have many cousins who look the same. You all look alike to me. Nice bird. Nice bird.

UNA: (Una returns looking refreshed but sad and has put on new lipstick) Jin will be home soon, Bruno. I hate to say it...but it is time for you to go.

BRUNO: I know. I know. When can I see you again, my dove?

UNA: (pauses a moment) How about next Wednesday night?

BRUNO: That long? I can't wait that long. By that time I will be desolate.

UNA: (grins) Bruno, we must be discreet. Besides, it is a lot cheaper here than...

BRUNO: Yes. Hotels get old after awhile. My place is surrounded with nosy neighbors who watch my every move.

UNA: Then we must be discreet. Wednesday night Jin is taking a class in history at the university.

BRUNO: (puzzled) Why?

UNA: It enhances his background, more pay, etc. It begins next Wednesday night. I think it begins at six. I'll talk to you between now and then.

BRUNO: (sighs) Until then, hasta la vista, baby.

(they embrace)
UNA: Same to you, Bruno. We'll be in touch.

Scene 3

Jin's class at the university includes Moira.
Dr. Jack arrives to begin the class.

(With his hair parted in the middle and combed straight back on both sides, he is dressed in a black pin striped suit, red breast-pocket handkerchief, a diamond stick pin, and a diamond-studded horseshoe on his left little finger. At first, many do not notice his gold watch and fob or even his silver-trimmed gambler's hat and black round toe western boots.)

JIN: (referring to Dr. Jack, looks at Moira) Who is this?
MOIRA: (smiles) A stud. Just my type to horse around with.
JIN: (grins) You tell 'em, Toots.
          (The class quiets down.)
JACK: Good evening everyone. This is a class in the history of Western America. In case you're supposed to be in another class such as calculus or astrophysics, this is a history course. Anybody in the wrong class?
          (one student gets up and leaves; to the leaving student, he waves goodbye) To continue, this class in Western American History is one that will focus on the Hollywood film industry. We will begin our study with a history of the development of the Hollywood star system, the role of the studios, and to write a research paper on some aspect of film or a particular movie star. First things first.
          (takes his pin striped coat off, rolls up his silk sleeves, revealing tatoos on his forearms, and sits at a table in front of the class)
          We will create a bibliography on all aspects of the Hollywood film industry---and there are thousands of books on this topic---as another project and goal of this class. I have selected aspects

of this topic and you can sign up for whatever part you want. It could be stars of the 1920's, the 1990's or the effect of Hollywood and the dreams it creates for those who want to try to make it big in the film industry. I'll pass this around.

(He passes the sign-up sheet around)

Another thing we will be doing is going every Wednesday night after our meeting as a class and going over a variety things on our weekly agenda, we will go over to the movie classics night in the little theater here on campus. What I want from you is to write a one page piece about one of the stars or a history of this particular film, not only for other members of this small class, but also the other members of the university or general public who will be attending that particular movie. You will then hand them out at the door prior to the beginning of the film.

Our first film next Wednesday night will be a 1998 release called *Paulie: A Parrot's Tale* starring Gena Rowlands, Tony Shalhoub, and Cheech Marin. I need not remind you that if you keep up with this course on a weekly basis, you can do very well. The topic is delightful, especially since I have spent time in Hollywood, met a few of the stars, had a few good times with them, etc, etc. On the other hand, putting it off, not bothering to do the work of the course, could be more like Custer's Last Fight. But this is true in any course, in any job, for that matter.

Your first assignment will be to sign up for a particular aspect of the Hollywood film industry, go to the library here and begin an alphabetically arranged bibliography of all works pertaining to that subject area. For example, let's say you choose Mae West or Clark Gable. Research every book written about either Mae West or Clark Gable and put those titles in alphabetical order. That way, by the end of the term we will have a very large bibliography. The schedule of films we will be viewing is also here on the table. Please pick one up on your way out. There are a variety of films this semester, including *San Francisco* (about the 1906 earthquake); *Doctor Zhivago* (we'll see how a physician and poet tries to survive a time of revolution); *It Happened One Night* (or what happened when the walls of Jericho come tumbling down between Clark Gable and Claudette Colbert); *Jaws* or how a Great White shark attacks at random off a quaint resort town), *The Long, Hot Summer* (where William Faulkner takes us on a tour of what it was like to live in Will Varner's Frenchman's Bend), *The Maltese Falcon* (the further sleuth adventures of Dashiel Hammett), *Some Like It Hot* (here we find out about the Milk Fund), *The Wild Bunch*, *The Dead Poet's Society* (or what it is like to take poetry and the lives of poets seriously) and so, before we meet again, I would like someone to volunteer for next week's movie which will be *Paulie: A Parrot's Tale.*

MOIRA: (raises her hand) I will.

JACK: Your name?

MOIRA: Moira Teodora.

JACK: Okay, Ms. Teodora —

MOIRA: It's *Miss* Teodora.

JACK: Fine. *Miss* Teodora. You can see me after class. I'll give you some more information on the kind of one-page presentation for next week. (to the class) If there are any questions, please see me after class. I'll see you next week.

(the class begins to file out)

Scene 4

Jin's apartment. Una and Bruno embrace.

UNA: You've got to go.

BRUNO: When will I see you again?

UNA: We'll be in touch.

(Bruno leaves. Una begins straightening up the bedroom and begins freshening up. Later...a knock at the door. Una looks concerned and puzzled. She goes to the door.)

UNA: Who is it?

POLO: It's me. Polo.

(Una opens the door.)

UNA: What are *you* doing here? You're not supposed to be here. Jin's on his way home.

POLO: Can I come in?

UNA: I'd rather you not come in.

POLO: Why? I haven't seen you in several days. Are you avoiding me?

UNA: Of course not. I've been busy.

POLO: Watching TV?

UNA: No. And I don't like your tone of voice, Polo.

LAM: (clears his throat) I love Polo. Arroz con Polo.

UNA: (with a louder voice so Lam can hear her) I told you to stay on the lam, Lam. And it's pollo, not polo. It's Spanish.

LAM: Pollo, not polo. He, he, he.

POLO: Quit changing the subject, Una. Are you avoiding me?

UNA: No. But I don't like your tone of voice.

POLO: (looks disgusted) Do I have no say-so in your life?

UNA: Of course you do. This is not a good time for us to see each other.

POLO: (walks upstage) Yet you have time for the man I just saw leaving this apartment...Who is he?

UNA: (embarrassed and fuming) None of your business! Are you spying on me?

POLO: (looking at the audience) Who is he? You can't answer?

LAM: (clears his throat and quotes) "There once was a gaucho named Bruno..."

UNA: (enraged) Shut up, Lam! Shut up! I mean it!

(Lam goes silent)

POLO: A gaucho named Bruno? The guy who left a note under your door that time? Is that him? (turns and looks at her) He doesn't look like a gaucho.

UNA: (fuming) It's time for you to go, Polo. It's time for you to go. Now. Jin is on his way home. He should be here any minute.

POLO: (mildly menacing) I'll be in touch.

UNA: You must go. Now. (heads backstage) Out this way. I don't want to take a chance with Jin coming home. Go down the fire escape. It is safe and easy.

POLO: I'll call you.

UNA: No more spying, Polo. Never again.

POLO: I'll call you.
    (Polo exits)

Scene 5

Jin's Apartment

UNA: (sighs) I'd better straighten this place up. (She begins making the bed and dusting. The sound of the door being unlocked is heard. Jin comes in.)

JIN: Honey, I'm home.

UNA: Welcome home. (gives him a kiss)

JIN: Am I glad to be home since there was quite a wreck down on Jefferson Boulevard. You know where it intersects with Hemmings Parkway?

UNA: Yes? What happened?

JIN: A big rig. I'm sure it'll be on the news. Why don't we turn on the evening news?

UNA: Sure. Why not? (She gets the remote and turns on the TV) How was your class?

JIN: It was something. (stops) Do we have anything to eat? I'm famished.

UNA: There's some left over Arroz con Pollo.

LAM: I love polo.

UNA: (rolls her eyes) That's enough, Lam!

JIN: (smiles) Nothing like a sports enthusiast. Maybe I'll warm some up. (Goes into the kitchen, gets some food, and returns) Oh, yes, the class. Looks like a winner. I never thought Western American history could be this interesting. We'll be learning about Hollywood, its history, the star system, the studios).

UNA: That does sound interesting.

JIN: And the professor is quite a work of art.

UNA: What do you mean?

JIN: Interesting dresser. Looks like a matinee idol from the 30s and 40s. Hair's parted down the middle. Well-trimmed mustache. Wears a western suit. Not like a cowboy riding the range, but very cosmopolitan western wear. Tatoos on his arms. Laser-like wit. Had this diamond horseshoe ring on his finger.

UNA: (absorbed by Jin's description) Really.

JIN: It's hard to believe. (drinks from his brew)

UNA: Anyone in the class you know?

JIN: Yes. Now that you mention it. There's a lady...

UNA: A lady? (seems concerned) What lady?

JIN: A lady that always comes by the park and wants her fortune read.

UNA: Oh, the one we've talked about before. What's she doing in the class?

JIN: I don't know. She may be just there because she's interested. She doesn't strike me as a student.

UNA: (a bit puzzled) I guess it's possible.

JIN: Just to take a course because you like it? Sure. Of course. Some people love to learn.

UNA: I haven't met many of those.

JIN: I admit. She *is* unusual. She always seems to be around.

UNA: Even at the park.

JIN: Yes, even there. (looks at TV) Oh, look, an interview. Look at the wreck. Awful. Bloody.

UNA: Yes, look at it. They're interviewing some people.

JIN: (with a surprised look) Hey, I've seen that guy. He comes to the park. Always wants to talk about fortunes.

UNA: (trying not to sound surprised) Oh, he does?

JIN: Yes, he likes to give us a bad time. Doesn't believe in fortune telling. He always questions our whole enterprise. Says it's all fake.

UNA: Do you know his name?

JIN: No, I've never asked. I just see him around a lot.

UNA: (relieved) Where have you seen him?

JIN: Other than at the park, I haven't seen him. Maybe somewhere else, too. I just can't recall where.

UNA: (relieved) Oh.

ACT III

Scene 1

Jin is asleep and Una is in a deeper sleep and sleeps throughout this scene. Jin is dreaming about Una. A woman resembling Una, whose name is Chance, appears on stage disguised as Fortune.

JIN: (somewhere between waking, sleeping and dreaming) Who are you?

FORTUNE: Who do you think I am?

JIN: Una?

FORTUNE: Yes, but not as you believe. In some ways, I resemble Una. But I am someone else.

JIN: Who?

FORTUNE: Fortune.

JIN: Fortune? Baloney. This is crazy. I don't understand.

FORTUNE: You will. You will see how closely we resemble each other.

JIN: I still don't understand.

FORTUNE: In the course of time you will.

JIN: Where is Una? I want just her in my dream. Her alone. Not you. Not someone masquerading as Una.

FORTUNE: You can't dictate who is in your dreams.

JIN: Yes, I can. Leave. Leave now.

FORTUNE: I told you how closely I resemble Una.

JIN: You can leave now.

FORTUNE: Only if you wake up.

JIN: No, I want you, I mean Una, to stay.

FORTUNE: You can call me Fortune if you wish.

JIN: No, I will call you Una. I do not want *you* in my dreams.

FORTUNE: (in a tone of command) I will be in your dreams…whether you like it or not.

JIN: (after a moment) What is it that you want?

FORTUNE: To talk to you…about things.

JIN: (wary) What things?

FORTUNE: (matter of factly) Oh, about what you want out of your life?

JIN: What I want? I'll tell you what I want. To be left alone. That's it. To be left alone.

FORTUNE: Oh, I think you want more out of life than that!

JIN: How come you think you know so much... about my life?

FORTUNE: I told you. I *am* Fortune.

JIN: That's right. Excuse me. And I am Freud. Sigmund Freud.

FORTUNE: You have a sense of humor...even in your dreams.

JIN: You got that right.

FORTUNE: But even your sense of humor cannot answer all of your needs. Isn't that right?

JIN: I did not say it could. (after a pause) Just what is it that you want to talk about?

UNA: Since I am Fortune, and not Una, I think you should know your fate.

JIN: So Fortune and fate are the same? I don't think so.

UNA: So you don't believe in Fortune or fate?

JIN: No. It is just a game. Another language game you're playing.

UNA: (with a frown) You think I am just a game player? That this is all a charade? You and Lam at the park every weekend? Isn't that deceiving people? All for money?

JIN: I am not a politician. Just a teacher and a business man.

UNA: Same difference.

JIN: I also teach philosophy.

UNA: Sometimes equally culpable. Although I do have a soft spot for the Liar Paradox.

JIN: Get off it, Una... What are you trying to do? Falsify my every statement?

UNA: Not at all. Besides, not everything you say is true.

JIN: Surely you have better things to do with your time than to intervene in my dreams...

UNA: There's no better time spent than time telling the truth.

JIN: Go ahead. Tell me the truth and let me return to my dreams of my darling Una.

UNA: I don't know whether it is better to tell the truth or simply to show it.

JIN: Ah, decisions, decisions! I would like you out of my dreams. If you have a truth to tell, tell it. Or show it. I am tired of your intervention.

UNA: But it's the knowledge I want you to have.

JIN: Whether it is truth or knowledge or knowledge of the truth…at this point I don't care. Just get on with it. I would like to get some sleep and continue my dream.

UNA: But there is a distinction between truth and knowledge of truth.

JIN: Next you'll be telling me not to plant the tree of the knowledge of good and evil. How's that for your keeping me in your dream of my longing for truth!

UNA: I'll just tell you, Jin. There must be separation for there to be good and evil. But here is your fortune, compliments of yours truly, Madama Fortuna.

JIN: Go right ahead.

UNA: I must tell you, Jin. This is not a good place for you. You are being deceived on a daily basis.

JIN: And how am I being deceived?

UNA: Your current loves are not your final ones.

JIN: What are you doing? Fortune telling? Funny how familiar I am with that!

UNA: That's what I do.

JIN: But everyone knows how fickle you are. One day yes, one day no, the next day, arbitration.

UNA: A raw deal if I've ever heard one. An undeserved reputation! I just try to help people with their futures. Not just their gold futures.

JIN: Yes, but—

UNA: No buts about it, Señor.

JIN: Still. That's how you are known. You *are* fickle. If you are Fortune, you *are* fickle. No doubt about it.

UNA: My, my, aren't we the final authority on how dice is played in the cosmos!

JIN: I'm not claiming final authority. I just know what I know. And if you are Fortune, you are fickle. There's no stability with you. You jitterbug with chaos.

UNA: And you know how good a dancer he is. (with swaying hands and hips motion) Hip hop, tango, fox trot, rumba. It's order that steps on my toes. She's not as good a dancer.

JIN: Ha! You change faster than old Proteus in Greek myth, that's what you do!

UNA: Well, I know what I know: your current loves are not your final ones.

JIN: I am so relieved to hear you reading my life lines.

UNA: You will appreciate my concern for your fate one day.

JIN: Maybe so. But Fortune, you are not my fate, I tell you. I just want to get back to my dream.

UNA: (mimicking with hands on hips) I just want to get back to my dream. (more serious) In a way...I am your fate.

JIN: (throws his hands up in the air) Oh brother, I am going back to my dream. You can jibber jabber all you want about fate and fortune.

UNA: (disgusted) It is not jibber jabber, believe me. You'll find out. Your fate, Jin, is not to take my words seriously.

JIN: Thank you! I'm going back to sleep. And to dream of my love. (looks at Una) She sleeps so peacefully while all this has been going on.

UNA: I am amazed she can sleep so peacefully. Especially with the fingerprints of fate all over both of you.

JIN: What's that supposed to mean? And fate's not on you?

UNA: (matter of factly) We are all fated in some way.

JIN: Whether in the words of awakening. Or in sleepy words.

UNA: (adding) Or in words from dreams.

JIN: I'd like to go back to my dream now...if you don't mind.

UNA: But you still haven't taken my fortune for you at all seriously. Once you do, I'll leave you to your dreams.

JIN: (frustrated) Thank God, I'm almost awake! I ought to let you have it!

UNA: (mildly warning) Don't tempt the fates.

JIN: And here I thought you were Fortune! (after a moment) Tell me, what is the significance of your fortune? "Your current loves are not your final ones." Tell me that!

UNA: As I said before, you are being deceived.

JIN: (resigned) I suppose I should be grateful. Well I'm not. I want to get back to my dreams. You can leave anytime.

UNA: As you wish, Jin. (exits)

LAM: (in a low tone from his cage) Here begin the sorrows of Jin.

Scene 2

That morning Jin and Una wake up about the same time.

UNA: (kisses Jin) You have a good night's sleep?

JIN: (yawns) I tried to. It was a strange night.

UNA: It was for me too. Strange indeed. I had a weird dream.

JIN: (matter of factly) Yes, tell me about it.

UNA: All right, I will. In the dream—you could call it a nightmare—I was being chased by a set of hands.

JIN: (with a puzzled look) Hands? Hands? What kind of hands?

UNA: It was like a bear was after me.

JIN: (makes a skeptical face) A bear? With claws?

UNA: No, they were hands. Not claws.

JIN: Where *was* this?

UNA: In the woods.

JIN: That figures. That's usually where bears are.

UNA: No, this was different. The woods were dark. I felt lost. Yet there was a door. I couldn't get it open.

JIN: (with a skeptical look) And the door was in the woods? It just happened to be in the woods.

UNA: Yes. It was at the far end. There was light coming from it. That's why I noticed it in the first place.

JIN: So, you were lost in the woods. You found a door you could not open. And a bear was chasing you. Is that right?

UNA: Yes. That's right.

JIN: (after a pause) Was the bear growling at you?

UNA: No, not really.

JIN: Not really? The bear was not growling.

UNA: No. He spoke to me. (Jin shakes his head) I know this sounds crazy. But he *did* speak to me. Honest he did.

JIN: (looks almost relieved as well as skeptical at the audience) I'm glad this is only a dream. Or maybe a nightmare. (a pause) Did the bear have anything to say?

UNA: No, no. I didn't think you'd take this seriously. You're laughing at me!

JIN: No, I am not. I'm not.

UNA: He kept saying the word Kama. Or maybe it was Karma. Over and over again.

JIN: (thoughtfully) How interesting. And Kama is?

UNA: Sexual desire.

JIN: And karma is…

UNA: (with a sigh) the consequences of our actions. The way this bear was chasing me…I figured he wanted to play me at least one hand.

JIN: It sounds like neither one of you was playing with a full deck. (after a pause) So, what happened? Did you ever get the door open?

UNA: Yes. It took forever. At first it…well the wind was blowing, almost howling. I thought the gusts would send me flying back toward the bear. But it didn't. It was so strange. Almost suddenly it stopped.

JIN: (with wonder on his face) Then what?

UNA: There was nothing. I could not see anything. It was like a sheet and so very still.

JIN: There was nothing?

UNA: Nothing. I couldn't see anything. It was like a fog. Covered with clouds. You couldn't see anything.

JIN: What about the bear? Was it still chasing you?

UNA: No. It was running but not running.

JIN: Not running?

UNA: I know it sounds weird. It kept moving but it was running in place. Going nowhere.

JIN: That is strange. Very strange indeed. (thoughtfully)

UNA: Acting like some medicine man. Some shaman. That's what it was like.

JIN: Strange that a bear would act like a medicine man. Some weird dream.

UNA: You're telling me. (after a pause) Why don't we get something to eat?

JIN: Let's do.

       (They exit offstage right)

Scene 3

The following evening.
Jin has left for class. Una lets Bruno in at the door.

UNA: It is so good to see you, Bruno.

LAM: Especially a gaucho named Bruno.

UNA: Shut up, Lam!

BRUNO: Ever feisty, Lam!

UNA: It is so good to see you! (they embrace)

LAM: (quoting) "There once was a gaucho named Bruno…"

BRUNO: Your parrot doesn't miss a thing! He's an intelligent bird, isn't he?

UNA: Unfortunately…he's too intelligent for his own good. (menacingly) I said shut up, Lam or I'm gonna put the cover over your cage! (turning back to Bruno) Now where were we? (They kiss some more)

BRUNO: It has been desolation to be without you. You know my love.

LAM: You can bet your sweet tootsies! (quotes) "Lola is fine and Carmen divine"

UNA: I said shut up, Lam! (to Bruno) Where is he getting such nonsense?

BRUNO: (shrugs) Beats me.

UNA: (goes to the cage and covers it) Take that, bird brain!

BRUNO: (frowns) You don't have to be so harsh. He's just a smart bird. That's all.

UNA: Well, I don't want to spend our time together talking about that parrot! He's so intrusive. And nosy!

BRUNO: He does have an inquisitive mind. Not many birds have that. (turns to Una; they deeply embrace)

UNA: You know my love for you, Bruno.

BRUNO: Time's a wastin'. (They head for the bed; they have just climbed under the covers when there is a knock at the door)

UNA: (whispers) Who could that be?

BRUNO: (whispers) How would I know? (there is another knock, this time a bit louder)

UNA: (Una gets out of bed and puts on a robe; she pauses, listening, then whispers to Bruno) Maybe they'll go away. (there is another knock, this time even louder) Maybe you ought to go. Go down the fire escape. It's safe and easy.

(Bruno gets out of bed and heads to the fire escape and leaves)

UNA: (listens and waits for another knock on the door; it is silent; she moves to the door and listens intently; a puzzled look comes on her face; she hears footsteps; Polo knocks at the door)
Who is it?

POLO: It's Polo. Can I come in?

UNA: (with an angry look) What do you want?

POLO: A chance to see my love again.

UNA: We had an agreement, Polo. You always call first.

POLO: I was in the area. So I thought I would drop by.

UNA: I'm expecting Jin any minute. You'd better go. Call me tomorrow. In the afternoon.

POLO: No, I want to see you. It has been torture these past few days.

UNA: This is not a good time, Polo. I'm expecting Jin to show up.

LAM: (quoting) "There once was a gaucho named —"

UNA: (interrupting) Shut up, Lam! (to Polo) Call me tomorrow, Polo.

POLO: I have to see you, Una. It has been too long, too many days and hours.

UNA: Call me tomorrow, Polo. If you don't leave now, you won't see me even tomorrow!

POLO: Okay, okay. I'll call tomorrow. (exits)

UNA: (fuming at Lam and lifting the cover) I'd like to string you up, Lam! How dare you mention a gaucho named Bruno.

LAM: Heh, heh, heh. I didn't mention Bruno, remember?

UNA: I think Jin should clip your wings and sell you. You are a dirty bird! A filthy rotten bird! A bird brain!

LAM: (remains quiet)

UNA: I've got to do something about Polo. He's intruding on my life! I want to do what I want when I want to do it. Polo's becoming a real pain! And so are you, Lam! (shakes her fist at Lam)

Scene 4

Jin and Moira walking toward Jin's apartment.

JIN: You did great tonight, Toots. A fine report on *Paulie: A Parrot's Tale,* background of the actors, and then we watched Paulie, a smart parrot!

MOIRA: It is a unique film! I think parrots are smarter than we give them credit for.

JIN: And Paulie had such a private life.

MOIRA: Indeed. It is something that fascinates me. You have to learn to listen. So much we screen out in order not to listen to anyone. Not talk to anyone.

JIN: You have a point there. Even a parrot has much to teach us.

MOIRA: But the person who keeps me interested is not just Paulie. It's Dr. Jack.

JIN: How do you mean?

MOIRA: It is like he has lived many lives. He talks about his wild days in Hollywood.

JIN: I have to admit he *is* colorful.

MOIRA: How many teachers have you had who wear pin striped suits and a diamond horseshoe on their little finger?

JIN: Not many. In fact, none.

MOIRA: That's what I mean! And last week! He talks about the stars as though he knew them. Remember his anecdotes about Lana Turner and Mae West? He's much more than a teacher, at least to me.

JIN: He seems to have a kind of empathy or sympathy to the stars he talks about.

MOIRA: Yes, he does. It's like he's lived many lives. A man of mystery and inherently interesting. (pauses) Anyway, see you this weekend.

JIN: Yes. I gotta head home. See you later.

Scene 5

At the fire escape to the side of Jin's apartment.
Enter Polo who has watched Bruno come down the fire escape.

POLO: (to Bruno) Hey you.

BRUNO: (Bruno turns around) Who me?

POLO: Yes, you.

BRUNO: What is it?

POLO: I just saw you come down that fire escape.

BRUNO: Yes I did.

POLO: Was there a fire?

BRUNO: No, not really. Not the usual kind.

POLO: Why did you come down the fire escape then?

BRUNO: (irritated) That's none of your business.

POLO: It *is* my business.

BRUNO: (starts to go) I said it's *none* of your business.

POLO: (grabs Bruno by the arm) It *is* my business. Might you be a gaucho?

BRUNO: (turns around after removing Bruno's arm) Years ago I was. I haven't been a gaucho in years. What business is it of yours? What's going on here?

POLO: You know a woman named Una who lives in these apartments?

113

BRUNO: And if I do? So what if I do? She's an old friend. She has many old friends.

POLO: She sure does.

BRUNO: What do you mean by that?

POLO: I know her too. And I've come down that fire escape before when her boyfriend, the guy she lives with, was coming home.

BRUNO: (his face turns pale with surprise) (aside to audience: I see why it's called a fire escape.)

POLO: Appropriate name, don't you think?

BRUNO: What?

POLO: Fire escape.

BRUNO: Yes. Yes I do. Especially if you're escaping fires. (pauses) You must be the guy she's trying to avoid.

POLO: What do you mean by that?

BRUNO: Just what I said. She says there's a guy who keeps following her, keeps trying to see her.

POLO: I do try to see her. I love her.

BRUNO: (with a smirk) I don't think she loves you. (pauses) She loves me. Not you.

POLO: (clenches his fist) Take that back! She's lying to you, too!
(They get into a brief wrestling match)
(Jin has put something in the garbage can and overhears their quarrel and wrestling)

JIN: Hey what's going on here? (He manages to pull them apart)

POLO: Nothing! Why don't you butt out of here?

JIN: Because you're disturbing the neighborhood. Not to mention my girlfriend.

BRUNO: Yeah, this is none of your business!

JIN: We'll let the police decide that. (He heads off)

POLO: I'll see *you* later. (In a huff, they go off stage in opposite directions).

Scene 6

Jin comes in, tells Una what has happened; Una feigns ignorance.

JIN: Hi, honey, I'm home. (puts down his briefcase)

UNA: Hello, Sweetheart. (they hug) (pause) How was your class?

JIN: Outstanding. (sits down on the couch; turns on the TV with a remote)

UNA: Oh, yeah?

JIN: It was great. And insightful.

UNA: How so?

JIN: Before we get into that...did you hear the noise outside?

UNA: Noise?

JIN: As I came up to the apartment, two guys were fighting.

UNA: Really? Two guys?

JIN: Two grown men. And they didn't like me. (pauses) Let me get a soda from the fridge. (he gets up and goes into the kitchen)

UNA: (she frowns) Do you know them?

JIN: No. Wait a minute. I've seen one of them before. Remember the guy who comes to the fortune booth on the weekends?

UNA: Who doesn't like his fortune? Wants to argue with you all the time?

JIN: (takes a drink) That's him. Always dissatisfied with his fortunes. Wants to quibble all the time.

UNA: Yes, I remember him. Black hair.

LAM: Yes, I remember him too! He, he, he, he.

UNA: Quiet, Lam! This doesn't concern you! We're talking, not you!

LAM: (aside) Oh, yes it does! He, he, he, he, he.

JIN: Well, he was one of the two fighting outside. I just stopped by to put something in the garbage can... and there they were. Fighting and calling each other names like 'liar for hire' and 'stench from the bog' etcetera.

UNA: 'Stench from the bog'? What on earth could that mean?

LAM: Gawd blimey, it's getting a bit slimey!

UNA: That's enough from you, Lam! (she goes into the other room and covers Lam's cage) We've heard enough from you. Go parrot someone else's lines!

JIN: Don't be so hard on him, Una. I just saw a wonderful movie tonight called *Paulie: A Parrot's Tale*.

UNA: I'd like to pull some feathers out of his tail when he butts into our conversation the way he does.

JIN: (takes another swallow) It does become a nuisance. But—

UNA: No buts about it. He has to learn not to butt into people's conversations.

JIN: (after a pause) You remember Moira? From the park? Loves Lam's fortunes but doesn't—

UNA: take them seriously. Yes, I remember.

JIN: Well, as it turns out she did a marvelous presentation on *Paulie*. Dr. Jack really liked it. Then we all went to the theater to watch the film.

UNA: Sounds like a successful night for Moira.

JIN: You bet. A roaring river success, I'd say.

UNA: (after a pause as Jin scanned the channels with the remote)
What did you find so interesting about *Paulie*.

JIN: The kind of life a bird can lead. He's a human bird. Only he chooses the people he will talk to. He's smart and savvy. Know what I mean?

UNA: He's very literate from what I remember.

JIN: Most definitely.

UNA: (tries to keep Jin on the subject of Paulie and not have him call the police) Even knows Chekhov and Tolstoy.

JIN: Indeed he does. An accomplished bird. He reminded me of Lam, our accomplished parrot.

UNA: (disgusted) He's accomplished all right.

JIN: I just remembered I was going to call the police.

UNA: Oh, don't bother. They'll just take a description and we won't hear anything more about it.

JIN: I would rather just snuggle with you. We can call
them later.
(Jin responds when Una kisses him; they embrace)

(Lights Fade)

ACT IV

Scene 1

Lillebonne Park. Enter Moira (later Polo)
(people are milling about, some in line for a fortune)

JIN: (to a customer) That's fine. This parrot is quite good at selecting fortunes. You want to try? (customer pays and Lam selects her fortune) (customer smiles and walks away with a hint of recognition of the fortune's accuracy)

JIN: Okay. Next? Ah, a favorite customer! Isn't that right, Lam? (Lam nods)

MOIRA: Indeed. Nothing like a fortune to get the day started. Here's my money.

JIN: All right, Lam. Your time to select.
(Lam moves along rows of fortunes and finally settles on one; Jin takes it from Lam's beak and hands it to Moira)

MOIRA: (after reading the fortune) That's something to think about.

JIN: A good one I hope.

MOIRA: Could be. Could be.

JIN: (looks puzzled) I thought you think this whole fortune-telling enterprise is foolish, Moira. You look like you're taking it seriously.

MOIRA: It *is* silly. I should not take it seriously. Especially since fate factors into the equations of our little lives.

JIN: Well, that must be a memorable one. You mind sharing it? What does it say?

MOIRA: It says: "Most of what happens is invisible to the eye."

JIN: That's not bad. Not bad at all.

MOIRA: I did not say it was bad.

JIN: Who knows maybe fortune can say something important about fate. I always think of your name, Moira, and what it means. And as the fates in Greek myth.

118

MOIRA: I'm sure between fortune and fate we can discover much.

JIN: (after a pause) Did your fortune have anything of a philosophical nature? Lam always includes something like that. It gives a different perspective.

MOIRA: Yes, it does have something down here. (she reads) "If ontology does not include ethics, your philosophy is still green." (looks puzzled) What on earth does that mean?

JIN: I assume it means that if the ethical, in other words your actions toward yourself and others are not good and just, then all your insights into the basic stuff of life are a bit shallow. (to Lam) Is that right, Lam?

LAM: You're getting smarter by the moment, Jin. And you too, Moira.

MOIRA: Ah, 'tis nice to be complimented by such a wise and smart parrot.

JIN: Not bad for a parrot trained in philosophy.

MOIRA: Not bad at all. I am more impressed by Lam the more I'm around him. Thanks, Jin. I'll have to think about all this. Ooops, someone's waiting. (Polo steps up to the booth)

JIN: (frowns) Yes, would you like a fortune?

POLO: Why not? I always get the worst ones. (hands Jin the money; Lam selects a fortune; Jin gives it to Polo who reads it)

JIN: A good one this time?

POLO: No, I told you I get the worst ones.

JIN: Sorry about that. You want to share it?

POLO: (thinks a minute) I guesso. This is what it says: "Seek a solution to your situation. Try to resolve it." I told you I always get the worst.

JIN: That's not necessarily bad. There's a philosophical part of the fortune, too. Is that also bad?

POLO: I don't know.

JIN: Well, what does it say?

POLO: (reads) Not real helpful. "Your character is your fortune."

JIN: It does not sound necessarily bad. It is simply an observation. An eyeful, you might say.

POLO: Don't kid around with me. Your whole enterprise is fake. These fortunes don't apply to me. That is why they are false.

JIN: You don't have to take them that seriously. (becoming disgusted) By the way, what were you doing fighting by my apartment the other night?

POLO: That's none of your business.

JIN: Actually it is my business. I get along with my neighbors. And to have people fighting and name-calling is a nuisance. Next time, I'm calling the cops.

POLO: You do that and I'll let them know you and your fortune-telling parrot are a fraud. People pay you and your parrot here for two-bit fortunes.

JIN: (to Lam) What do you think of that Lam?

LAM: Like it says: "Your fortune is your character."

POLO: (disgusted) Shut up, bird brain! I should've known better to come here. Here's my fortune for you: "You both are living a lie. Open your eyes and ears."

JIN: (waves him on as the next person in line steps up) Remember what I said about fighting.

POLO: (as he goes off) And you remember about living a lie.

Scene 2

At home Jin tells Una about confrontation with Polo; Una is concerned.

JIN: Honey, I'm home.

UNA: Hello, my love. (they kiss) And how was your day at the park?

JIN: Business was fine. People are fascinated by Lam's fortunes. Anything for dinner? Something smells good.

UNA: One of your favorites. Arroz con Pollo.

LAM: The old Arroz con Pollo ploy.

120

JIN: That's enough, Lam.

UNA: That *is* enough, Lam.

JIN: I'm hungry already. (after hanging up his coat, turns on the TV, begins trying to find out what is on TV)

UNA: What would you like to drink, Jin?

JIN: Just a soda. (He surfs the TV channels) Not much on tonight. I'm really tired for some reason.

UNA: There should be a good movie on.

JIN: Any polo matches?

UNA: I don't think so.

LAM: (has been listening) Did you say polo?

UNA: Quiet Lam! You don't have to repeat everything you hear.

JIN: But that's his nature. He learns in depth through repetition.

UNA: But he doesn't have to repeat *everything*.

LAM: You mean like "There once was a gaucho named Bruno..."

UNA: That's enough, Lam! I swear Jamaican me crazy! (she puts her head in her hands)

JIN: Now, now. Okay, Lam. That's enough. You know when enough is enough.

LAM: I sure do. Enough is enough. (tilts his head as he eyes Jin)

UNA: (after a pause) As I was saying, there might be a good movie on.

JIN: (Una brings in the food; Jin continues cruising the channels)
        With all these channels, you'd think there would be more than a wasteland on the tube. No polo, no soccer. Mostly reruns.

UNA: Wait. What was that? A movie classic. *Some Like It Hot.*

JIN: Tony Curtis and Marilyn Monroe? Let's see it.

UNA: We can make it a movie night.

JIN: I don't know if I will make it through the movie. I am tired. And it still bothers me that this guy that I've told you about before came up and griped about his fortune.

UNA: What about his fortune?

JIN: As usual, he didn't like it.

UNA: The same guy?

JIN: The same guy.

UNA: What's the problem now?

JIN: He said the fortune was false. Improbable. And that Lam and I were cheating the public.

UNA: What was the fortune?

JIN: It simply read: 'Your character is your fortune.'

UNA: What bothered him about that?

JIN: He took it personally. (after taking a sip from his soda) When you think about it, it does make sense.

UNA: (concerned) How so?

JIN: We can't escape our character. We are who we are.

UNA: But character can change, don't you think?

JIN: Not really. A leopard may change her spots but she's still a leopard.

UNA: Why do you say "she"? I hope you're not referring to me?

JIN: (surprised) Not at all! It just came out that way.

UNA: (self-conscious) I may be like a leopard, but I do change my spots now and then.

JIN: I didn't mean to imply you were a leopard. It was just an illustration. It was not meant for you personally! This guy is not going to ruin my evening with you. If he doesn't like his fortune, that's the way it goes.

UNA: I agree. (pause)

JIN: Something else does bother me though. Turns out he was one of those two guys fighting outside the apartment awhile back. He was not happy when I brought up that fact.

UNA: (concerned) Oh, you did? What happened?

JIN: As usual, he comes up and asks for a fortune. I have no idea why he does that since he then claims that the whole thing is false, a fake business, and berates the process, me and Lam.

UNA: I don't understand that either. If he doesn't believe there's any truth to it, why does he even bother?

JIN: That's something I don't understand either. I have students like that.

UNA: Not everybody likes to know their fortune. Or the truth, for that matter.

JIN: No kidding. Like I said, he gets his fortune and reads it. As expected, he does not like it, claims that it is false.

UNA: OK. Then what?

JIN: I asked him what he was doing fighting outside our apartment building.

UNA: (concerned) What did he say?

JIN: Told me it was none of my business. I said 'Oh, yes it is.'

UNA: What happened next?

JIN: I had to wave him off. Customers were waiting.

UNA: Good idea. No use trying to argue with him. Sounds like his character really *is* his fortune.

JIN: I think you're right. (after a pause)

UNA: (changes the subject) How do you like the Arroz con Pollo?

JIN: (eats a forkful) Ummm Umm. Deeelicious. As always!

UNA: Let's watch the rest of *Some Like It Hot*.

JIN: Good idea. Let's. (They continue to eat as the movie comes on)

(Lights Fade)

Scene 3

Days later. Jin is at his class.
As usual Dr. Jack is dressed in a dapper way.

JACK: (claps with students after a presentation is made on *It Happened OneNight*) Nice presentation on Gable and Colbert, stars of our movie tonight at the little theater, *It Happened One Night*. We'll get a chance to see what happens when the Wall of Jericho comes tumbling down between the heiress played by Claudette Colbert and the newspaperman played by Clark Gable.

(Moira raises her hand)

JACK: Yes, Moira.

MOIRA: Are we still going to have a one-page profile on each of them tonight?

JACK: Yes, the students who have done that-let's see (looks at his class roster) that would be Cambria for Gable and let's see Olaf for Colbert. I assume you both are ready? (the two students nod) Good. You can pass those out when we get to the theater. You should go now since the movie begins in twenty minutes. (the two students leave with papers in hand). Oh, before I forget, I've appreciated the bibliographies you've been working on. The history of the star system in Hollywood is especially impressive. By the end of the semester, we'll have a thick, authoritative bibliography on most phases of the Hollywood film industry.

(Jin raises his hand)

JIN: Dr. Jack, I've been researching the literary genealogy of five characters in *Gone With the Wind*. So far, only Rhett Butler is an original character in Southern literature. Should I still include the other characters anyway?

JACK: Yes, go ahead. I'd include them anyway. I'd focus on Butler and what makes him unique.

JIN: Will do.

JACK: If there's no more questions, why don't we mosey on over to the little theater and take our seats. Be sure to get the program profile from Olaf and Cambria. (The class gets up and files out; Moira and Jin walk together; Jin motions for her to slow down and let the others go on)

MOIRA: What is it? We'll be late.

JIN: I'm not feeling too good. You go on. I'll give Una a call. Maybe we have something at the apartment that will help with my upset stomach. You go on, Moira. You can tell me all about *It Happened One*

Night. I want to know all about it. I'm sure Dr. Jack will grill us next week.

(takes out his cell phone and calls Una; the line is busy)

MOIRA: You sure?

JIN: Might know it. The line's busy. Yes, you go on. I'll talk to you sometime before then. Remember, I want to know all about it.

MOIRA: Sure thing. Hope you feel better.

(they exit)

Scene 4

Enter Polo at Una's door; she is on the phone when she comes to the door.

UNA: (on the phone opens the door; she frowns when she sees Polo) I'll call you back (hangs up the phone) What are *you* doing here? I told you to get out Polo and not to come back!

POLO: I know. I know. But I just had to see you again.

UNA: You've seen me. Now beat it troublemaker!

POLO: (begins trying to push open the door) Let me in, Una. I want to come back!

UNA: But I don't want you back. And you know why! If you don't stop pushing on this door, I'll scream!

POLO: (after a pause) You wouldn't dare! I'll just tell everyone what's been going on here!

UNA: (pushes the door back at Polo) You do and you're finished! I mean it!

POLO: No, *you're* finished! You brought this on yourself!

UNA: Just go. Beat it, troublemaker! Go now. Leave!

POLO: But I want to see you!

UNA: I've seen enough of you to last a hundred lifetimes! Now go!

(enter Jin who sees Polo at the door who then backs off; Una is shocked to see Jin)

UNA: (to Jin) What're you doing home?

JIN: I wasn't feeling too well. I called a couple of times but the line was busy.

JIN: (to Polo) What're you doing here? Did you come by to complain? You can do that at the Park. I'll be there on Saturday.

POLO: (smirks at Una; then to Jin) Good. I'll be there.
(Polo leaves; Jin comes in; Una is very concerned)

UNA: So what is going on? Are you sick?

JIN: I don't know. I just didn't feel well. I lasted until the class was to go over to the little theater. I just came home. Moira will tell me what went on.

UNA: But isn't that part of your grade?

JIN: Yes, but if you don't feel well...I don't see the point.

UNA: (she puts his coat in the closet and takes off his shoes) What movie will you miss?

JIN: It's called *It Happened One Night.*

UNA: Oh, yes. That's the one with Clark Gable. I always liked him.

JIN: Moira will tell me all about it. I'm sure Dr. Jack will understand.

UNA: Can I get you anything? Something to drink?

JIN: Sure, ice cold beer. (Una goes into the kitchen) By the way, what on earth was this guy doing here? First he's in a fight with another guy. I have to threaten to call the cops on 'em. Then he comes to the Park and insults our fortune-telling parrot. He insults Lam. I'm sure the bird's feelings were hurt. Now he comes over to this apartment again and is raising a commotion at our door. What is wrong with that guy?

UNA: He's just is some poor unfortunate who spends his days bitching about everything. Some people are not happy unless there's something to complain about.

JIN: I've seen his kind before, believe me. (Una hands him a beer)
I think we should call the cops on him. That's twice he's been here; now to complain. Some people have a lot of gall!

UNA: They certainly do.

LAM: Yes, they certainly do. He, he, he, he, he, he.

UNA: Quiet, Lam! I should've known that bird has been listening. I'll hear about it for days, no doubt!
(the phone rings; Una quickly gets up to answer it)

JIN: I've gotta to see a man about a horse. (points) To the bathroom.
(Jin goes upstage and picks up the extension and listens to the conversation)

UNA: I can't talk now. He's home and doesn't feel well.

JIN: (frowns then says aside) Who could this guy be?

UNA: All right then. Maybe tomorrow. (hangs up)

JIN: (pretends he is coming from bathroom) Who was that, honey?

UNA: Just one of my girlfriends. Wanted to talk the night away. She can call back tomorrow.

JIN: I see. (he seems to accept what she says at face value)
(they begin to watch TV)

JIN: (after a pause) I don't know what it is but I'm still not feeling that well.

UNA: Can I get you anything else?

JIN: No. I'll go lie down.
(Jin leaves; Una is alone; Lam is listening)

UNA: What am I going to do? I don't trust Polo. He's too jealous. And belligerent. I love Bruno. And Jin for that matter. Everything's closing in.

LAM: (aside) Unfortunately, truth is sometimes elusive and hard to bear.

(Lights Fade)

Scene 5

Next day. Jin is at home.
Una has gone to get groceries.
Jin and Lam have a revealing conversation.

JIN: (turns on TV remote as he lies on the couch) There must be something on. A polo match! Yes, the Dan Bruno Gauchos!

LAM: Did you say Gauchos?

JIN: Of course, Lam. You heard me! A Gaucho's match!

LAM: I already know a gaucho named Bruno.

JIN: (looks puzzled) Lam, I'm trying to watch this. We can talk later.

LAM: "There once was a gaucho named Bruno, who said "there's one thing I do know that Lola is fine and Carmen divine-"

JIN: (interrupting) Lam, can't you see I'm trying to watch this match? I'm not feeling all that great!

LAM: (in a softer voice) "But Una is numero Uno"

JIN: (pause for a commercial) Okay, Lam. There's a commercial on. Now what were you babbling about?

LAM: Just a limerick I learned.

JIN: How does it go?

LAM: Are you sure you want to know?

JIN: Since there's at least eight commercials...go on. I'll put them on mute. Now, go ahead. With your limerick.

LAM: "There once was a gaucho named Bruno, who said "there's one thing I do know that Lola is fine and Carmen divine but Una is numero Uno"

JIN: (puzzled) Where on earth did you learn that? Was that limerick in one of your fortunes? You certainly didn't learn it in philosophy class unless you've been taking a correspondence course in the philosophy of the body.

LAM: (wistful) No, it's in one of *your* fortunes.

JIN: (more puzzled) What? A limerick? How can that be? I've never heard it before. You know how fortunes can be repetitive. They're like body types or memory muscle fed by reflex milk.

LAM: Let's not get too elaborate.

JIN: I'm just trying to make a point.

LAM: And I'm trying to tell a fortune.

JIN: My fortune? You're trying to tell *my* fortune?

LAM: You bet.

JIN: What I want to know is...where did you learn that limerick? And who is a gaucho named Bruno?

LAM: I learned it from him?

JIN: You learned it from a gaucho named Bruno. Where? At the park?

LAM: No, he told it to me. Right here.

JIN: In this apartment?

LAM: Right here. In the apartment.

JIN: (puzzled) When did you learn it?

LAM: A few weeks ago.

JIN: (puzzled) In this apartment?

LAM: He's the one in the accident.

JIN: What accident?

LAM: The wreck. He saw it.

JIN: (puzzled) A wreck?

LAM: At the intersection of Hemmings and Jefferson.

JIN: (recognition) Ah! Oh, yes. I remember! He was in the wreck?

LAM: No, he saw it. They talked to him.

JIN: I know who you mean. He was fighting out here one night with a guy named..what's his name? Uh.

LAM: Polo.

JIN: That's right. Polo. So the guy who taught you the limerick is named Bruno?
(he thinks a moment)

LAM: That's right. I haven't seen him at the park. But he has been here several times.

JIN: What's he been doing here?

LAM: If you can't figure that out, you're no philosopher!

JIN: That is one helluva misfortune, Lam.

LAM: Please don't say anything. It's all I can do to survive around you know who.

JIN: You'd better not be making this up, Lam. Or you'll be a ham on the lam. Permanently.

LAM: I am well aware the truth is hard to bear.

JIN: (rubs his jaws thoughtfully) I'll tell you what... I want you to recite the limerick when she's around. I want to see her reaction.

LAM: Are you kidding? My life will be worth nothing! Please don't ask such a thing! I'm sure she will say I'm making it up! Please don't ask me to do such a thing!

JIN: I'll protect you, Lam. You're safe with me.

LAM: But you're not around all the time! She *is*. And she'd like to have me on a skewer as it is!

JIN: Trust me, Lam. I just want to find out what's going on.

LAM: I can tell you what's been going on. She's been seeing two guys behind your back.

JIN: These are serious accusations, Lam.

LAM: Truth is hard to bear. Truth is hard to hear.

JIN: You're good at telling fortunes. But the truth?

LAM: If I am lying, then--

JIN: Then what?

LAM: You can sell me or give me away! But what I tell you is true.

JIN: (rubs his chin) If what you say is true, I will be devastated. She's my love, my life.

LAM: You may be devastated but I would rather know the truth, however painful it may be.

JIN: You're just saying that. That would be years of my life, down the tubes!

LAM: But isn't it better to know the truth? It can make us free, you know.

JIN: I've taught you well. You have a decent grounding in philosophy.

LAM: You're not so bad yourself.
(just then Una comes to the door; she is carrying a bag of groceries)

JIN: Here lemme help you.

UNA: Could you get the milk and the carrots, too?

JIN: Of course.
(Jin helps her with the groceries)

UNA: You feeling any better?

JIN: Not really.

UNA: (puzzled) Just put the peanut butter over there in the cupboard. Not feeling well? Still your stomach?

JIN: A little bit of that. Just not feeling all that good.

UNA: Thanks, I'll put these cold cuts in the fridge. If you could put the raisins and the spices away. That'll help. Go ahead and sit down. Can I get you anything?

JIN: No, I'll get something cold.

(he sits down; Lam can be seen in the next room, tilting his head to listen)

JIN: (sits glumly)

UNA: (turns on the TV, notices Jin's mood) Anything wrong?

JIN: I'm a bit concerned.

UNA: About what?

JIN: About you and I.

UNA: (concerned) You and I?

JIN: Yes. Could you turn the TV down?

UNA: But it's my favorite cooking show!

JIN: Not to turn it down might be a recipe for disaster.

UNA: Disaster? What?

JIN: We have to talk.

UNA: About what?

JIN: You and I, as I said before.

UNA: Go ahead.

JIN: (sighs) Do you know a man named Bruno?

UNA: Who wants to know?

JIN: I do. Do you know such a man?

UNA: I know many men.

LAM: You ain't just a whistlin' Dixie, Bruda!

JIN: Stay out of this, Lam. Do you know a man named Bruno?

UNA: Yeah. Yes, I do.

JIN: Does he happen to be a gaucho?

UNA: A gaucho? He might have been at one time.

JIN: Has he ever been over here?

UNA: (frowns) I resent your tone of voice, Jin! Are you accusing me of something?

JIN: All I did was ask a question. Has he ever been over here?

UNA: He may have been by. Why do you ask?

JIN: Why would he come by?

UNA: (pauses) He's a painter. And looking for a model.

JIN: A painter? Why would he ask you? Are you known in the world of painting?

UNA: I've modeled before. Long ago. He contacted me because of a mutual friend.

JIN: A mutual friend?

UNA: Yes.

JIN: Who?

UNA: I feel like I'm being interrogated! Can we change the subject?

JIN: No, I have to find out a few things.

UNA: I'm missing my favorite cooking show!

JIN: I don't care if you're missing your mind. I want to know some things.

UNA: (surprised and exasperated; throws her hands up) Go ahead! Fire away! The mutual friend is a banker named Polo.

JIN: A banker?

UNA: Bruno was interested in a loan.

JIN: And Polo was the person to make the loan?

UNA: That's right.

JIN: So Polo the banker referred Bruno the painter to you?

UNA: More or less!

JIN: Yes or no.

UNA: Yes.

JIN: And you declined to be Bruno's model?

UNA: That's right.

JIN: (pauses thoughtfully) Did he want to paint you anyway?

UNA: Yes. But I told him I was not interested.

JIN: You mean, like a portrait?

UNA: That's right. He had some kind of Modigliani or Picasso fantasy.

JIN: So, Bruno's an aspiring painter?

UNA: That's right.

JIN: (pauses thoughtfully) Did he ever try to push it on you? Or pay you to model for him?

UNA: No. He accepted my decision not to pose for him. (a prolonged pause)

UNA: Any other questions?

JIN: Not right now.

UNA: I don't understand what all this is about.

JIN: I just have some questions. Some things to find out.

(Lights Fade)

Scene 6

Next day. Jin is at the park. Una calls Bruno; tells him to lay low. Polo comes by and is questioned by Jin.

JIN: Guess who's first, Lam. Our old friend Polo. For a guy who thinks this fortune telling business is fake, you sure are a frequent buyer.

POLO: My money's as good as anyone else's.

JIN: You want a fortune?

POLO: Why not? They're all fake. And what does your bird know?

JIN: He knows enough.
         (Polo pays Jin)

JIN: Okay, Lam. It's your choice. The man wants his fortune.
         (Lam picks one) There you go. (hands it to Polo)

POLO: (reads it and frowns)

JIN: Pretty awful, eh?

POLO: It doesn't apply to me.

JIN: Why, what does it say?

POLO: (reads) "Jealousy can be a recipe for disaster."

JIN: That's a pretty good fortune, Polo.

POLO: It doesn't apply to me.

JIN: Tell me, what does it say at the bottom? I'm always curious about tactful tidbits of philosophy there at the bottom.

POLO: (reads) "Ethics means not just to do our duty but to anticipate the consequences of our actions, given the situation" I told you, it does *not* apply to me.

JIN: Sometimes they're on target. Sometimes they're not. Here's your money back. I'm sure a big banker such as yourself needs all the cash you can muster.

POLO: (surprised) How do you know I'm a banker?

JIN: A little bird told me.

POLO: (eyeing Lam) Not that bird!

JIN: No, just my girl. Una.

POLO: (disturbed) Una?

JIN: Yeah, my girlfriend. She finally admitted some things.

POLO: What things?

JIN: Oh, you might say: "Your character is your fortune."

POLO: Clever! And so is your bird! Just remember my fortune to you: "You both are living a lie."

JIN: And how is that?

POLO: Una and I go back a long way. She's my love of loves.

JIN: Is that so? How so?

POLO: We met a long time ago.

JIN: Is that when you were going to loan money to a painter named Bruno?

POLO: A painter? A pain you mean! No, I wouldn't loan a cent to Bruno. He's so smug!

JIN: So you don't like Bruno?

POLO: Can't stand him. And he's not a painter! He's simply in the business of being in business.

JIN: She told me you loaned money to Bruno to support his painting.

POLO: I don't believe it. She's been making it with Bruno for a long time. Like I said: "You both are living a lie."

JIN: (pause in shock) Is Bruno the guy you were fighting with that night?

POLO: He was coming down the fire escape courtesy of Una. And I confronted him. He said Una loved him, not me. So we fought.

JIN: That sheds some light on things.

POLO: Now you know how she has played you for a fool.

JIN: And you too. And you too. (sees a customer coming to the booth) I have other people who want their fortunes. I'm sure I'll see you again.

POLO: You better believe it.

(Lights Fade)

Scene 7

Jin and Lam come home. Una is filing her nails and reading a fashion magazine.

JIN: Honey, I'm home.
UNA: (gives him a hug and kiss) How was the day for you?
JIN: The park was at times busy. Really busy.
UNA: Everybody like their fortunes?
JIN: Everybody except one.
UNA: Don't tell me.
JIN: (nods) The chronic complainer.
UNA: I'm surprised.
JIN: I was too.
UNA: So did he call your enterprise a fake?
JIN: The usual. He got a fortune he didn't like and said it didn't apply to him.
UNA: I'm curious. What was the fortune this time?
JIN: Something like "Jealousy can bring on disaster."
UNA: Really. And what was his response?
JIN: The usual. It didn't apply to him.
UNA: (smirks) Nothing ever applies to him. Isn't it amazing? Nothing. No fortune ever applies to him.
JIN: That's what he always says.
UNA: Did he stomp off at that point like he usually does?
JIN: No, I mentioned to him that a banker such as himself should invest in something he actually believes in.
UNA: (concerned) You mentioned he's a banker?
JIN: Yes, that's what you told me.
UNA: (gets up and paces around) You didn't have to mention that!
JIN: Why not? It's the truth, isn't it?
UNA: Why yes it is. It is the truth.
JIN: But you know what else I found out?
UNA: (interjecting) Can't we watch my favorite cooking show?
JIN: No, not right now. Please. There's too many pots on the stove as it is.
UNA: Okay. What else did you find out?

JIN: I found out he can't stand Bruno. That he wouldn't loan a cent to Bruno and that Bruno is not even a painter.

UNA: That liar! Polo is lying to you! I'm going to give him a call.

JIN: You don't have to do that.

UNA: No, I'm going to.

JIN: You know his number?

UNA: (taken aback) Why yes.

JIN: Why? Why do you know his number?

UNA: Just in case.

JIN: Just in case?

UNA: Just in case he spreads lies about me.

JIN: What about Bruno? He denies Bruno is a painter.

LAM: (interjects) And Bruno can paint anyone into a corner!

UNA: For the last time, Lam. Shut up! I just want to give him an earful!

JIN: But we're not finished, Una. Polo also said he loves you and that you both go a long way back. (Una paces nervously)

UNA: That liar! Wait till I get a hold of him. That liar!

JIN: So you don't go back a long way?

UNA: Of course not.
(Una continues to pace nervously)

JIN: Does he love you?

UNA: No comment.

JIN: No comment? You have no idea?

UNA: I don't want to talk about it.
(after a long pause)

JIN: I've been doing a lot of thinking.

UNA: I don't want to go there. I don't like your tone of voice.

JIN: As much as I regret to say this...

UNA: (runs and hugs him) Don't say anything you'll regret.

JIN: (gently undoes her arms around him) You need to go.

UNA: To leave? You want me to leave? To move out?

JIN: (nods) Yes. It's best. For both of us. My heart is breaking.

UNA: Doesn't sound like it to me.

JIN: Trust me. It is.

UNA: So you're taking the word of a banker? Of Polo? And his hostility toward Bruno?

JIN: Let's say it is putting two and two together. A pair of insights that have been in plain sight so long I could not see them.

UNA: So you want me to leave? But I love you, Jin. We had...

JIN: I love you too! For so long. But here the road diverges. You have your way. (Jin's eyes become teary)

LAM: Here begin the sorrows of Jin.

UNA: For once you got something right, Lam. But you conveniently forgot my sorrows.

LAM: The ones you created?

UNA: I didn't create them? It's just a convenient stroke of fate.

LAM: Or fortune!

UNA: Baloney! What would you know? You're just a meddling parrot!

JIN: Yet Lam is one of the few truth tellers around!

UNA: What?!

JIN: Yes, Lam here alerted me along time ago. I just didn't see it. Didn't want to see it.

UNA: What? Through a limerick?

JIN: You could say that. Because I didn't teach him the limerick. It had to be someone other than you or me.

UNA: He could've heard it *anywhere*. Most likely at the park.

JIN: If so, I would've been next to him to hear it.

UNA: (to Lam) Where did you hear the limerick?

LAM: From a gaucho. Named Bruno.

UNA: Baloney! You made it up! You meddling parrot!

LAM: He stood next to this cage and recited it.

UNA: I don't believe you.

LAM: He said: "There once was a gaucho named Bruno
(that's me) who said 'There's one thing I do know:
That Lola is fine and Carmen divine
But Una is numero Uno.'"

JIN: And here's where you heard it?

LAM: You betta believe it.

UNA: (stares at the parrot and into space) I'll have to
talk to him about that.

JIN: You'll have to go.

UNA: Where will I go? I can't go back to mother's house.

JIN: There's always Polo or Bruno.

UNA: A pox on both of their houses!
(Una begins gathering her clothes together)

(Lights Fade)

Scene 8

Moira and Jin walk home from his class.

MOIRA: I'm sorry to hear about it. Of course it's
devastating.

JIN: She was my life, my love. I just detest investing that
much time in a relationship with all that going on.

MOIRA: Of course. But isn't it better to know this now?

JIN: (glum) I suppose so. You love someone and they
can still be callous and unaware.

MOIRA: I agree. What if it had been your misfortune to
have children with her and be married with all
the family. It would have been even harder to
deal with.

JIN: You have a point there. I probably should be
celebrating. But my heart's not in it.

MOIRA: The celebrating will come later. Let time
take its course. Someday you may thank your
lucky stars...

JIN: Or my good fortune.

MOIRA: It's fated despite the moves of our moving fingers.
(they pause ready to go in different directions)

JIN: Thanks for listening. And for being a friend.

MOIRA: And being mine. See you next week. Call if you
want to talk.

Scene 9

Jin and Lam back home.

JIN: Well, Lam, I've finished grading exams. Why
don't we watch some TV. No soccer tonight. How
about a movie called *A Man and A Woman*?

LAM: That might be depressing. I've watched you mope
around these past weeks. Not a good choice.

JIN: You're right. How about the *Wild Bunch*? Naw.
On second thought I'm not much in the mood for
a western.
(continues turning the channels with the remote)

LAM: Is there any exciting movie?

JIN: Here's one. *Zorba the Greek*. With Anthony Quinn.

LAM: A good choice!

JIN: I feel like dancing already! (finds the channel)

LAM: This will help get your spirits up!

JIN: (feeds a treat to Lam) Yes it will.

LAM: You're in a better mood already! I can taste it.

JIN: I like the way Zorba teaches his boss how to dance!

LAM: A fantastic way to go!

JIN: (brings in a sandwich and beer and begins
watching the movie)
A great fortune-telling friend.
(Jin toasts Lam) Here's looking at you, Lam. I wish
you only good fortune.

LAM: And you too! And you too! May it be our fates to
have good fortune. (winks at Jin and the audience)

(Lights Fade)

THE END

Smokescreens

a play in one act

Cast of Characters

MRS. O: nickname of a retired clerk in her mid-80s who rents part of her old house to Chris Perl.

CHRIS PERL: freelance writer and tenant in the house owned by Mrs. O.

PAULA ALALU: substitute teacher and fiancée of Chris Perl

STEVE HIMMEL;
LORETTA MULDOON; }
ANGEL RAMIREZ } local police officers in this small California town

BROWN GOODMAN alias KEGGER DUDE (non-speaking character)

Scene

Chris Perl's rented room. He and Paula are in a prolonged embrace. The phone rings. In a daze, Chris answers it.

Time

The year is 2001.

Scene 1

CHRIS: Hello. Oh, it's you, Mrs. O. No, no, it's not too late. What's on your mind? Oh (his voice falls). You think they're out there? (He frowns at Paula gravely).

Okay. I'll come over. But I can't be there as long as last time. Fine. See you then. (He hangs up). It's 2:31 a.m. and she wants me to come over.

PAULA: Why?

CHRIS: You know why. Periodically she thinks someone is under the house or on the property.

PAULA: Don't tell me you're going again? (She looks incredulously).

CHRIS: (frowning) I told her I would. She thinks they're under the house...blowing marijuana smoke into her bedroom. And she won't let anyone into her bedroom to smell it.

PAULA: Under the house? (incredulous; Chris nods) Under _this_ house? Right now?

CHRIS: (nods in a dazed way) I know. I know. I've told her many times. No one's under the house. But she insists.

PAULA: Can't you tell her there is no one?

CHRIS: I have. Many times.

PAULA: (frustrated) So we give up our evenings so your landlady can have you come over to find whoever she thinks is under the house. Who are they this time?

CHRIS: The Dude family. (a pause)

PAULA: And last time?

CHRIS: The Zooey family from down on Randolph Street.

PAULA: At that rate she should be able to blanket the town. (Chris puts on his jacket and with a high-powered flashlight, leaves. Paula turns on the TV.)

PAULA: Don't stay out too late, deary. (Chris smiles and goes down the stairs and out into the driveway leading to Mrs. O's portion of the old house. She is wearing a dark blue shawl under the porch light. In her mid-80s she is a

141

large-boned woman, matronly, opinionated and kind. Her dress is handmade with modest faded denim ruffles.)

CHRIS: (as though routinely) Where do you say they are?

MRS. O: Right there. I think they go in through that hole.

CHRIS: (frowns then smirks) We're not talking about gophers, Mrs. O.

MRS. O: I was thinking of rats.

CHRIS: (frowns) We've looked in there before. The opening has not been touched. It is only eighteen by fifteen inches. It has a screen. (on his knees with his flashlight) You see (turns off his flashlight) there's no one in there. What makes you think anyone's there?

MRS. O: The noise, the marijuana smoke.

CHRIS: Pot smoke? I don't smell any kind of smoke. How do you know it's marijuana smoke?

MRS. O: I once chaperoned a rock concert by Cannibal Corpse. I was high by the time it was over. And…I wasn't smoking anything!

MRS. O: Someone's there, I tell you, Chris. There's more smoke here than meets the eye.

CHRIS: (aside) Smoke _and_ mirrors. (then to Mrs. O) We've been over this before. No one is that small. Not even Dudes. This screen hasn't been touched.

MRS. O: Chris, I tell you by all that's true and holy, there is a Dude under the house.

CHRIS: Really, there's no one under this house. No one's that small. (He gets on his knees again and turns on the high beam of his flashlight.) No, there's no one under your house. And, to be honest Mrs. O, I don't smell smoke either.

MRS. O: Well, I heard some of these punks around here today.

CHRIS: Hmm. Who were they?

MRS. O: That family I was telling you about. The one I caught trespassing in the backyard that time.

CHRIS: Did they have marijuana?

MRS. O: I don't know. They kept saying something about Acapulco Gold.

CHRIS: It is getting kind of late. Almost three o'clock. Could we discuss this tomorrow?

(Mrs. O nods and goes inside).

MRS. O: Sure. Thanks, Chris. I'll call if I hear them again.

Scene 2

The next evening. Chris is reading. Paula stops drying dishes.

PAULA: I don't know how you put up with it.

CHRIS: (looking up) Mrs. O? (Paula nods.) She's always been kind to me. Even reduced my rent. How often does that happen? And besides, she <u>is</u> getting old...

PAULA: I'll say...

CHRIS: She's already eighty-five...and hard of hearing.

PAULA: It can't be that bad if she hears people on her property. She has no reservations about including anyone she doesn't like.

CHRIS: She says she's had skirmishes with them before.

PAULA: Who specifically?

CHRIS: She's mentioned them before. A family down the street...she says the older boy, Kegger, not the younger boy, Gunnar, has thrown rocks at the house. He runs around with some rowdies or, as she calls them, punks. They've thrown bottles on her lawn and made all kinds of noise. She calls the cops on 'em. She says the Dudes are like that...the Zooeys too for that matter.

PAULA: So she thinks they come over here to smoke pot to get back at her?

CHRIS: Yes. Probably.

(Just then the phone rings)

CHRIS: Hello. Oh, hello officer. What? She has? Sure. Hang on. (puts the phone down; he goes out the door and returns in a moment) Hello. Officer Muldoon. No. I looked. There's no one on the property that I can see. Okay. Sure. Will do. (He hangs up the phone. Then to Paula) She's called the cops.

The officer wanted---(he phone rings again) This should be interesting. Hello. Oh, Mrs. O, hello. You did what? Uh...huh. What did they say? No, I'm sure they're not just taking a prolonged coffee break...when they should be out catching punks and hoodlums...No, I'm sure they'll take care of it. No. I wouldn't call up the cops and say they are 'lazy louts who are talking to their fiancés on precinct time.' No, that wouldn't be a good idea, Mrs. O. Really it wouldn't.

(Paula's hand is over her mouth)

No, no. Calling the cops 'Lazy bums' is not a smooth move either. Cops have a hard life as it is, you know...The stress of the job. Just like mob bosses. What's that? Sure, I'll keep an ear to the ground. If I hear anything, I'll go out and investigate. Sure, Mrs. O. You have my word on it. Goodnight. (He hangs up the phone)

PAULA: A direct pipeline to the Police Department. It doesn't sound like she thinks too highly of them.

CHRIS: No. She thinks they don't spend enough time investigating all the people who are under her house smoking pot.

PAULA: I can't imagine why. As if the cops had nothing better to do.

CHRIS: If you believe her, the cops don't even do their jobs. They just sit around and drink coffee. Play pinochle. Solitaire. Talk to their fiancées on the phone.

PAULA: (shaking her head) Incredible.

CHRIS: (with a laugh) Yes. It truly is. And it doesn't help that she tells them off each time they refuse to come out here and search the place. (pause) I've talked to Officer Muldoon before. She specializes in talking with her on the phone. She must be assigned to that detail. She gives Muldoon an earful. The doctors, politicians, plumbers, people who work at the deli. You name it. Imagine if the cops had to respond to every crank call...inspect every garden, every birdbath...

PAULA: Just imagine...there'd be no time for coffee breaks. Or tea time.

CHRIS: Or to be called 'lazy louts' or 'do-nothing punks on precinct time.' That one was Muldoon's favorite... 'do-nothing punks.'"
(Chris and Paula shake their heads with bemused grins).
It could be a long night.

Scene 3

The police station next morning.
Officer Muldoon chats with Officer Ramirez.

RAMIREZ: You must get tired of that woman calling up here. Calling us names.

MULDOON: I do.

RAMIREZ: It must get old.

MULDOON: Sure does. But since I'm a woman I don't get sent where the action is.

RAMIREZ: You'll get your chance.

MULDOON: (she looks skeptical) In the meantime, Mrs. O...
(They continue to do paper work, occasionally filing reports in an "out" bin on their desks)

RAMIREZ: (after a moment) 'do-nothing punks...'

MULDOON: You ought to hear her on the doctors... and the lawyers... who try to gouge everyone--- including people her age.

RAMIREZ: It must be...

MULDOON: What?

RAMIREZ: Lonely. Terribly lonely...to get old. To feel useless, isolated. To know your friends, people in your family are long gone. Not many of your own generation around anymore. Always new faces... new names. Pressures of another world. Another generation.

MULDOON: That's why I indulge her. Let her spout off.

RAMIREZ: Muldoon, I swear you're a saint ...
(Muldoon smiles)

145

MULDOON: You're no devil's advocate yourself, Angel.
    (Ramirez grins)

RAMIREZ: (after a pause) She have family?

MULDOON: Only a son-in-law…who wants her property once she's committed to a nursing home. Other than some friends…she does have a social worker but he gets upset with her bossiness. Mrs. O once even called the agency and asked them not to send him again. Her minister comes by. They get along. Mrs O. actually likes her…Probably because she knows how to listen. Sometimes people just want you to listen to them. So I let her have her say.

RAMIREZ: You're a saint, Loretta.
    (Officer Himmel arrives.)

HIMMEL: (Interrupting) Who's this?

MULDOON: Mrs. O.

HIMMEL: Oh, her again. She ought to be put in a nursing home. We can't waste office time with her illusions. Don't tell me she was bellyaching about someone on her property…what was it?… smoking pot?

MULDOON: Yes.

HIMMEL: What else is new? I say the old mare should be put out to pasture.

MULDOON: (Disgusted) Himmel, you're such a breath of fresh air.

HIMMEL: I tell it like I see it. She wastes our time with her phone calls, her imaginings. Take that time we actually drove out to her house. No one was on her lot at all. She was hysterical. Claiming someone was making noises, throwing bottles. And we went out there. Nothing. A waste of time. It costs money to send officers out on that kind of mission.

Scene 4

Chris Perl's room. In another room, Paula is listening to Charlie "Bird Man" Parker's rendition of "Ko-Ko."; Chris is writing. The phone rings.

CHRIS: Paula, would you turn off the music?

PAULA: You want me to turn off Charlie "Birdman" Parker?

CHRIS: Yes, I'm on the phone. (Paula turns off the music)

CHRIS: Hello. Oh, it's you, Mrs. O. How are things?

MRS. O: Not good, Chris. I keep hearing noises. And the smoke is really thick. I believe it's those Dudes again.

CHRIS: (sighs) Okay. Sure. I'll...I'll check it out.
(He hangs up the phone, sighs, and looks at Paula who rolls her eyes as he goes out the door. Mrs. O in a striped dress has come outside and stands beneath the porch light. Chris begins to search around the property. After several minutes...)

CHRIS: I don't see anyone, Mrs. O.

MRS. O: I just know it's that punk and his buddies... blowing marijuana smoke. How brazen they are!

CHRIS: (aside) And probably high. (serious) Try to calm down, Mrs. O. But...with all due respect...I don't see anyone on the property. (Mrs. O frowns, then changes the subject.)

MRS. O: The screen...has it been moved?

CHRIS: Not at all. Remember no one's that small. Especially a teenager. (after a pause) It *is* getting late, Mrs. O. Sorry. I really don't see anyone on the property.

MRS. O: Thanks Chris. We'll find these punks.
(She goes back inside; Chris shakes his head and returns to his room.)

PAULA: Find anyone?

CHRIS: What do you think? (with a sigh) It may be a long night. I'm getting older by the minute.

Scene 5

Early morning a few days later. Officers Muldoon, Ramirez, and Himmel have responded to a call from Mrs. O who claims there is an intruder on her property.

MULDOON: This should be interesting.

HIMMEL: Another time of waste and money.

MULDOON: I'm glad you're enthusiastic…and supportive.

HIMMEL: I just tell it like I see it.

MULDOON: Sometimes telling it like you see it is not enough. Maybe you don't see it at all.

HIMMEL: Let's not get into another argument about Mrs. O. You know what I think about her. That's that.

RAMIREZ: Yes, let's not—

MULDOON: We all know what you think. And you're probably right. But being right all the time is not always wise.

RAMIREZ: Amen.

HIMMEL: Let's drop it and go see Mrs. O's latest folly.

> (They drive on in silence. Himmel looks out the window in a distracted way as does Ramirez; Muldoon carefully pulls the squad car up along the sidewalk in front of Mrs. O's house. They get out. After Himmel talks to Chris who has been questioning the suspect, he comes over to Muldoon and Ramirez who have noted Mrs O's arrival.)

HIMMEL: Blondie over there was found drunk on Mrs. O's lawn.

MULDOON: Who is he?

HIMMEL: Says his name is Kegger…Kegger Dude.

> (Muldoon, and Ramirez give each other questioning looks)

MULDOON: *That's* Kegger Dude?

HIMMEL: Well, think what you want to think, our beachcomber here had a wild party last night. Must have danced till dawn. Then flopped out here.
> (Himmel picks up a bottle found with the suspect and sniffs it) Phew! Pretty bad stuff. (to Muldoon) Let's put him in the car.
> (Mrs. O leans over to Chris)

MRS. O: I told you. I told you.

CHRIS: (tries to calm Mrs. O) All right, Mrs. O. Still he was not smoking marijuana.

MRS. O: We don't know that.

CHRIS: In his condition? He'd be lucky to find a match!

HIMMEL: (to Mrs. O) They're running a background check right now.

MULDOON: (to Ramirez) He's not a Zooey or even a Dude. He's a surfer. That's all. And a drunk one at that. (whispers to Ramirez) I wonder why he's so far inland. These guys rarely leave the beach. (Ramirez shrugs his shoulders)

MRS. O: (with a righteous tone to Chris): I told you. Nobody believed me. The cops made fun of me. Those punks.

CHRIS: Please, Mrs. O, don't start name calling. Okay? Be glad they're here and got this guy in custody.

MRS. O: Some coffee ought to sober him up!

CHRIS: (whispers) Unless all of it was drunk at coffee break.

(Mrs. O grins with obvious relish)

PAULA: They can always make another pot. No pun intended!

(Muldoon gives a document to Himmel who peruses it.)

HIMMEL: Wait a minute. The name he gave…Kegger's just an alias.

RAMIREZ: No kidding.

HIMMEL: Says here he calls the Mendocino coast his home. Has been arrested before….mostly minor stuff. His real name is…Brown Goodman.

(All give each other quizzical looks).

HIMMEL: (to Mrs. O) There really _was_ someone on your property this time. I guess we owe you an apology. (pause) By the way, it would be nice, ma'am if you didn't refer to these officers as …"punks." We _are_ here to serve.

MRS. O: What? Coffee? Tea?

HIMMEL: Now, Mrs. O. We _did_ come out here. We've got the man in custody. Do you want to press charges?

MRS. O: (still not placated) Yes….on second thought… no.

HIMMEL: We'll check him out first. He'll have a fine to pay and then be on his way. (They get in the squad car and pull away from Mrs. O's house)

MRS. O: (laughs) Those cops. They just need some prodding to do their jobs.

CHRIS: Yes, but Mrs. O, this guy…what's his name?

PAULA: Brown Goodman. Hmmm. Not Young Goodman Brown as in the short stories of Nathaniel Hawthorne.

CHRIS: Oh, yes. He was *not* under your house. He was *not* blowing marijuana smoke either. Not even Maui Wowie. He was just on the front lawn. Remember that. You may have another visit from someone else sometime.

PAULA: This is just one person. One unfortunate.

MRS. O: I know. You don't believe me either. But it feels nice to show the cops they're not —

CHRIS: Mrs. O. We believe you-at least I do-otherwise I would not check under the house at all hours of the morning.

MRS. O: I know. I know. And I appreciate it. (a pause) You kids have a wonderful day.

(She heads back to the house with a distinct bounce in her step).

Scene 6

Officers Muldoon, Ramirez and Himmel in a conference at headquarters.

MULDOON: (notices Ramirez's smile) What are you smiling about?

RAMIREZ: I'm just glad he wasn't a Dude or a Zooey. You know how she thinks.

HIMMEL: (with disgust) Or doesn' t think. I'm just glad he wasn't blowing marijuana smoke into her house.

MULDOON: I'm just glad it was a he and <u>not</u> a she.

(Himmel rolls his eyes; Ramirez grins)

(Later…)

MULDOON: You know what I found out? I spoke to another officer…Atta Ajanaku…no, Whitecloud was his name. He said this guy…Brown… Goodman told him that if he was ever caught on Mrs. O's property...that he—get this—was to tell the cops his name was Kegger Dude. He agreed to tell us that was his name. Apparently that he's been around this neighborhood before. Many times.

HIMMEL: Surfing the neighborhood many times, eh?

MULDOON: (continues) Said he was told that—and he agreed—with Mrs. O. They actually had an agreement. Mrs. O and Brown Goodman.

RAMIREZ: To say he was Kegger Dude?

MULDOON: Yes.

HIMMEL: (dumbfounded) She just might be smarter than we think.

MULDOON: I'm afraid that tells the tale.

The Russian River Returns

a play in one act

Cast of Characters

JAMES NOGARTH: a learned man in his fifties
GEORGE NOGARTH: James' devil-may-care younger
    brother
ANITA FRANCESCI: longtime friend of both brothers
DAME LYDIA NOGARTH: mother of James and George

Scene

A two-story house on the Russian River in Northern
California.

Time

Mid-summer, the 1980's.

Scene 1

James and Anita on the sun deck overlooking the Russian River.

ANITA: You want some more water?

JAMES: No, not right now. (After a pause) Any word?

ANITA: No, no word. George said she'd be coming to town soon.

(For a moment she seems a bit far off.)

JAMES: What did he say?

ANITA: Who? (She snaps back into the present.)

JAMES: George.

ANITA: Oh. That your mother wanted to pay you a visit. It might be her last time in this neck of the woods.

JAMES: I'm sure it will be. Oooooh. Ooooooh.

(He says this faintly with a slight grimace of pain.)

ANITA: (Anita rushes to his side.) What is it sweetheart?

JAMES: The pain. It never ends.

(She sits next to him and begins stroking his hair. After awhile...)

JAMES: Why is she coming now? She's had the last twenty-two years.

ANITA: I wish I knew. I never quite understood her.

JAMES: She always liked the idea of you and I together. Married.

(Anita nods; her eyes drift far away.)

JAMES: You and I. (his voice drifts off as he stares out the window.)

ANITA: It could have been you know....

JAMES: Yes, I know. I know. That was a long time ago.

ANITA: What the years show us...reveal us as being... "all the choices spread out among the boulevards"...

(Her voice drifts off as she pauses in her stroking of his head.)

JAMES: (He nods faintly, occasionally grimaces with pain.) What's it like now?

ANITA: It?

JAMES: The river. It's too painful to sit up or even stand for long periods. I can see a little bit but not all of it.

ANITA: (She stands up to get a better view of the river.) The same.

JAMES: It can't be the same. Remember what Heraclitus said.

ANITA: Ah, yes, the philosopher. "We never step in the same river twice." Well, what I meant was it's still green as the oak trees next to it. The khaki hills, ravines hay-colored, baking in the sun...browning with the heat of summer.

JAMES: And hawks? Are hawks there?

ANITA: (She cranes her neck.) Yes. (She counts in a whisper.) Three. Yes, three of them. Circling and circling.

JAMES: And the people?

ANITA: Bathing. Some floating on air mattresses. Mostly kids. Oh, one's swimming from the dam to a little dock that has a red boat tied to it.

JAMES: That's the way I remember it. Even when overseas. (He breaks off, grimacing in pain.) You know, I don't think I should see her. I'm bad off enough.

ANITA: Just give her a chance. If she's nasty, I'll steer her out of here. Have her leave you alone. Okay?

JAMES: (nods faintly)

(Just then gravel-scrunching tires are heard from the driveway below.)

ANITA: Someone's here. (She goes to the window and peers out.) George is here.

(In a few moments James's brother, George, appears at the door. A burly man in his late forties, he is athletic, jovial, somewhat overbearing.)

GEORGE: Anybody home? (His voice booms to match his swagger.)

ANITA: Yes, in here. (He knocks.) George. Welcome. (She hugs him; he kisses her; finally she breaks away.)

GEORGE: How goes it, bro?

(He takes a chair by James and moves it close to him.)

JAMES: The same.

GEORGE: Still not up, eh? When are you going to get up and ride? Huh?

JAMES: (with an attempt at humor) Maybe next week.

GEORGE: Ah, that stuff's all in your mind. Ever since Hilda died.

ANITA: He's really sick, George. Really he is.

GEORGE: In his mind only. He just thinks he can't go on without her. Why she's been dead for two years now.

ANITA: He's got cancer, George. Here's the diagnosis if you don't believe--- (She shows him a document.)

GEORGE: (interrupting her) Purely psychosomatic. He's brought it on himself I betcha. And with you doting over him, he'll be in bed quite awhile.

ANITA: If you can't be nice, George, maybe you should leave.

GEORGE: Why don't you and I go? You know how I feel about you. For years...but you've spent all your time doting over a man (gestures toward James whose face is mapped with disgust) who married someone else. Good ole Hilda.

ANITA: (takes his arm) I think you ought to leave.

GEORGE: Protecting him to the end, eh?

ANITA: If I want to...it's none of your---

GEORGE: (interrupting her) One of these days you'll wake up...and discover your truelove loved you all along.

(He regards James.) You're the one who had all the advantages. College. Even a degree in philosophy! Talk about impractical!

JAMES: (waving away his words) Sorry you're so resentful. There's so little time, you know. Mother is coming.

GEORGE: Mother, eh? What would she want with you after all these years?

JAMES: I don't know. Maybe she wants to kick me one last time.

GEORGE: How like her! How very much like her!

(Just then from the gravel driveway below: the sound of tires crunching. Both George and Anita go to look out the window. Below, a silver-haired lady steps out of her car which is luxurious but obviously not of current vintage; slowly, inexorably, she makes her way to the house. Elegant, almost statuesque, her bearing exudes authority, a refinement with a surface veneer. Her gait is purposeful, strong.)

GEORGE: (to James) Guess who. Brace yourself. The Grand Dame cometh....

ANITA: She's here. I don't believe it.

Scene 2

Let in by the maid, Mrs. Lydia Nogarth, enters the house. Soon there is a knock at the door; Anita lets Lydia in. There is a long pause as if adjusting to a different light.

JAMES: (James has propped himself high on his pillow.) Hello mother.

LYDIA: Hello. (a long pause)

JAMES: It's been a long time.

LYDIA: Yes.

JAMES: Twenty-two years.

LYDIA: Yes. That's a long time.

JAMES: (changing the subject) You know she's dead.

LYDIA: Hilda?

JAMES: (nods)

LYDIA: Yes, I heard. (She says this with a tone of disdain.)

JAMES: It's been two years.

LYDIA: (out of James's hearing) Not long enough.
        (Then she changes the subject.) I see Anita's back in your life.

JAMES: (raises himself from his pillow) Yes, she is. And she's been wonderful.

LYDIA: (She glances at Anita whose eyes remain riveted to the floor; she seems somewhat annoyed Anita is still in the room.) I'm glad to hear that. (George's voice booms down the hallway.)

JAMES: (falls back into his pillow) Guess who.

LYDIA: My other darling, chief clown, always restless for what he can't have, a child dead with thirst... (Her voice drifts off.)

GEORGE: (After Anita lets him in, he says) Hello mother dear! (He gives her a bear hug.) Haven't seen you in a barrel of Tuesdays! You're even more stunning with the passing years!

LYDIA: (She gives him almost a disdainful smile but does return his hug.) Hello George.

GEORGE: You've come to see my dear bro? (Lydia nods.) I think all this is in his head, don't you?

LYDIA: I don't think so. Not this time. Not this time....my first born is....

GEORGE: I can't imagine it. He's had all the advantages.

LYDIA: You could've gone to college too. But you liked to party all the time.

GEORGE: Let's not get into that. (Then he changes the subject.) Anita, let's you and I go. You can make me some of those deeeeelicious cookies you used to make. What were they called? Oh, yes, I remember. They were called "Ain't These Tasty?" I really liked 'em. And they were tasty! Why don't we go make some?
(He tilts his head to indicate to her it is time for them to go.)

ANITA: Yes, why don't we. I'm sure they have some catching up to do.(They leave. Lydia crosses over to a chair and sits down. It too faces the river; they both stare at its waters for a few moments.)

LYDIA: (after a long reflection) It all comes to this.
(Her eyes look far away.)

JAMES: I guesso. All those years you could've seen me but didn't want to.

LYDIA: You know why. Look who you married.

JAMES: She was the rose at dawn, my lightworks, (and quoting) "my moon or more."

LYDIA: Hrmph. (with a tone of definitiveness) She was trash who stained the family name. (upset) All she ever did was divide us. Always tension in the air with her around.

JAMES: You just didn't like her. (matter of factly)

LYDIA: That's right. For what she did to you...

JAMES: To me? (then grimacing in pain) Ooooooh.

LYDIA: (pauses briefly) Yes. She took all your money.

JAMES: (shakes his head) No, she didn't.

LYDIA: Got you into drugs...made a living hell of your life...wearing leather pants all the time..tattoos all over her body...George told me all about it.

JAMES: (grimacing again) George doesn't know anything. He blathers---

LYDIA: (interrupting him) He knows enough. Then when you were arrested...that was the last straw... for me anyway.

JAMES: (occasionally grimaces as he stares at the river and its currents) That was based on lies...

LYDIA: I told you she was bad news from the very start. Even her family was trash. And all the while Anita was right here. All along you could've married her, had children, made something of yourself. But Hilda (she smirks saying this) was your one true love. How deluded could you be?

JAMES: (sighs and shrugs) That's all in the past. Can we talk about something else?

LYDIA: Not until I'm finished.

JAMES: (musters strength) Anita! Anita! Come in here! Anita!

(There follows the sound of running feet. Anita enters bewildered, not knowing what to expect.)

ANITA: (to James) You okay?

JAMES: She's upsetting me. Ooooooh. I don't want to hear anymore. I thought I could die in peace with you. But that's not going to happen. Please go.

(He waves his arm toward the door.)

LYDIA: Not until I'm finished.

(She moves toward James on the bed; Anita moves in between them.) Out of my way, Anita! This doesn't concern you.

ANITA: It does concern me. You're killing him.

LYDIA: Let's not be melodramatic. He killed himself long ago when he didn't marry you.

ANITA: (embarrassed) The past is past. Long ago. I must ask you to leave. (Anita holds Lydia's arm who abruptly pulls it away. Suddenly George knocks at the door.)

GEORGE: What's going on in there?

ANITA: Go away George. Just a discussion. If I need help, I'll call you, okay?

GEORGE: Okay. (his footsteps almost skip down the hallway.)

ANITA: (to Lydia) I must ask you to go.

LYDIA: (to James) You ruined everything. Just remember that.

ANITA: (takes Lydia by the arm; she struggles to get free) Let's go. He's had enough for today.

LYDIA: I've had enough for all time.

(Anita gets George to escort his mother home. The sound of Lydia's car diminishes in the distance. Anita returns.)

JAMES: (staring at the eddies and currents of the river) What a waste.

ANITA: Try not to talk.

JAMES: What a waste. She's never going to change. (He grimaces.) It was a mistake. Too much bitterness.

ANITA: (nodding) I know. (She sits by him stroking his hair.) Yes. How sad not to be accepted.

JAMES: (nods slowly) Sometimes. Sometimes. (Lying more flat now, he stares at the ceiling. After a pause, he clears his throat and speaks.) Tell me, what're they doing now?

ANITA: (looks up and down the beach) Some kids on inner tubes. (she smiles) Air mattresses. Can you hear them? Splashing. Kicking. Like we used to do.

JAMES: (with a faint distant smile) Yes. Like we used to do.

About the Author

Born in Honolulu, Richard Alan Bunch grew up in the Napa Valley. His poetry works include *Red Orchids and Daffodils*, *Third Eye of Nowhere*, *Running for Daybreak*, *Summer Hawk*, and *Rivers of the Sea*. He is the author of short stories such as "Veiled Interlude," "Kismet," "Whipped Cream," and "Music City Skyline." His plays such as *The Russian River Returns* and *The Fortune-Telling Parrot* have appeared in several venues. His poetry has appeared in *Poetry Cornwall*, *Fugue*, *Potpourri*, *Windsor Review*, *Albatross*, *Slant*, *Oregon Review*, *Poetry New Zealand*, *Hurricane Review*, *Poem*, *Many Mountains Moving*, *Red River Review*, *Slant*, *Homestead Review*, *Dirigible*, *Haight Ashbury Literary Journal*, *West Wind Review*, *Comstock Review*, *Cape Rock*, and the *Hawai'i Review*.

"(Bunch's) voice is wise and captivating, for many poems show him to be an intriguing poet with a keen connection to history, to contemporary culture, having an admirable seriousness of purpose."

— Jeffrey Levine, *Tupelo Press*

(Bunch's) poems are "well-written, richly evocative, and filled with compelling images."

— K.A. Hunter, *Carriage House Review*

Of *Collected Poems 1965-2011*:

A compendium of the poetry of Richard Alan Bunch, *Collected Poems 1965-2011* showcases more than 450 examples of his verse, some of which saw earlier publication in a variety of publications, some of which are published here for the first time. A literary and personal pleasure to browse, *Collected Poems 1965-2011* offers a variety of poetic forms and an impressive diversity of themes. If you can only find time in your present circumstances for one poetry anthology, you would be well advised to make it Richard Alan Bunch's *Collected Poems 1965-2011*!

— *Reviewer's Bookwatch*

CPSIA information can be obtained
at www.ICGtesting.com
Printed in the USA
FSOW02n0722300915
11676FS